LEADING
WITH
MY CHIN

JAY LENO
WITH BILL ZEHME

HarperCollins*Publishers*

HarperCollins books may be purchased for educational, business, or sales promotional use. For information please write: Special Markets Department, HarperCollins Publishers, Inc., 10 East 53rd Street, New York, NY 10022.

FIRST EDITION

Designed by Joseph Rutt

ISBN 0-06-018694-1

96 97 98 99 00 ❖/RRD 10 9 8 7 6 5 4 3 2 1

To my mother and father,
my brother, Pat, and all of my aunts and uncles
and other members of my family,
who made my childhood such a wonderful time
—and especially my wife, Mavis, whom I love very much,
for sharing a great ride and improving it with every mile
we've traveled together

CONTENTS

1

THE SEARCH FOR
THE SEVENTH MAN

Biologically speaking, I came late to the party. Which is to say, when I was born, my mother was forty-one and my dad was forty-two and my brother was already ten. I may not have gotten here on schedule, but at least I got here. This built-in generation gap probably defined me every bit as much as my distinctly peculiar blood mix. I'm a half-breed of the oddest sort: one part Scottish, one part Italian. The combination makes no sense. Because each side couldn't be more diametrically opposed. My mother, Catherine, was born in Scotland, and my father, Angelo, was a first-generation Italian-American. And I seem to be divided right down the middle. My Scottish side is practical, analytical, even a bit frugal. My Italian side is loud, outgoing, ready to laugh (and be laughed at).

Of course, my mother never really understood the Italian part of my behavior. When I was a boy, she would always scold me, "Now, there's a time to be *serious*—and a time to be *funny!*" But, in truth, there was *never* a time to be funny! We could be

1

at Disneyland and my mother would say, "Not now!" I'd say, "*Not now?* Mom, when am I supposed to be funny? We're at Disneyland!" It was always time to be serious. She would later watch me do my standup comedy and make little notes. I'd ask her how she liked the show. And she would consult her notes, then actually say, "You know, no one wants to see someone be funny *all the time.*" She'd say, "Why don't you tell some jokes, then maybe sing a little song or . . . do a little *dance!* Make it entertaining. Nobody wants to hear jokes *all the time.*"

The most entertaining spectacle of my youth was watching both sides of my family try to interact. Each side obviously had totally different attitudes and approaches to life. At the Italian functions on my father's side, there would be hundreds of meatballs made for maybe a dozen people. More food than anyone could possibly eat. Huge pots, huge portions. And my mother's sister, Aunt Nettie, would be incensed by this. "Oooh, look at the food that's goin' to *weeeeste!*" she'd say in her thick burr. "Oooh, the *weeeeste!*" If there were more than two lights burning in any room, she'd scream, "I can't believe it! All these lights on! The *weeeeste* of electricity!"

Then we'd go to Aunt Nettie's house, which was run on the safer side of frugality. I remember how she kept Coca-Cola in the cupboard, because to refrigerate even one bottle would somehow quadruple the cost of the electricity. There was nothing like the sound of a warm Coke being opened—sort of a long wheezing *sssssssss*—and then seeing it pour out all foam and no liquid. The foam, accompanied by a nice stale scone, made for a Scottish dream snack.

But my Aunt Nettie was a very lovely woman. She came to America just ahead of my mother, who followed at the age of fourteen and moved in with Nettie and her husband, Alex. Now, Uncle Alex was the classic Scotsman, by which I mean *extremely thrifty*. He liked keeping a close eye on his money. One time he fell down and lost consciousness for a few minutes. This was a big scare. My father was there and bent down to help. He shouted, "Give him some air!" Then he opened Alex's shirt and put his hand around the waist of his pants, trying to move him. At that moment, Alex snapped awake and started squeezing my dad's hand so hard that he almost broke it. He screamed, "You're not gettin' me wallet, Angus!" (My mom's family always called my dad Angus instead of Angelo; why, I don't know.) My father, of course, thought this was the funniest thing ever—that is, once he got some feeling back in his hand.

■ ■ ■

Later in my life, my mom tried to enforce the Scottish thriftiness upon me in the sneakiest ways. For instance, she never understood why an adult single man didn't save old french fry oil. Back at home, you could go down in the basement and find jars marked BACON FAT—1959. This, then, explained the mysterious appearance of the yellowy, grease-filled bottles I'd find in my cupboards during my parents' trips to see me in California. I'd say, "Mom, what am I gonna do with this stuff?" And she'd say, "Well, you never know when you might need it!" Like whenever I felt the overwhelming need to contract ptomaine poisoning!

I remember the first time they flew out here, she was just enthralled with the meal on the plane. She said, "Oh, the sandwich was so deee-licious, I asked the attendant to wrap up the other half for you." So she handed me this soggy napkin at the airport. I said, "Mom, I don't want an airline sandwich!"

She said, "Well, just put it in the icebox, anyway!" The sandwich stayed there for about a year and a half.

On their visits, Mom always insisted on cooking all the time, which seemed like a ridiculous way to spend a vacation. To give her a break, I'd usually just bring home Chinese food. And even this had horrible repercussions. She refused to throw out the unused little packets of hot mustard and soy sauce. Never mind that I had *bottles* of mustard and soy sauce! I'd start dumping them and she'd scream, "You're not going to throw that away!" So I'd keep these stupid things. Then whenever they left, I'd have this big purge of the kitchen, going through the drawers and cookie jars and scooping up *hundreds* of little packages of condiments and plastic forks. Then I'd mail them back home to her. You never knew when she might need them.

I'll never forget one horrific night when they were staying with me: I came in late and they'd already gone to sleep. On the way home, I'd stopped off to gather the ingredients for the perfect hamburger, which I loved to put together for myself. I'd gotten the freshly ground, incredibly lean meat at the special butcher. I'd gone to the best bakery for the rolls. And I also bought a new bottle of Heinz ketchup, because I thought we were all out.

But once I got home, I opened the refrigerator and saw a half-bottle of ketchup. I didn't think twice about it. "Fine, I'll use that," I thought. I always prefer the chilled ketchup, anyway. So I made the hamburger, toasted the bun, put the burger on it. Now for the final touch on my perfect burger—ketchup. I tipped the bottle over it. *Splash!!!* It came like a gusher! *Tomato water!* I couldn't believe the devastation! It soaked the meat and disintegrated the bun, and I started yelling and screaming, like I'd been stabbed: "*Aaaaaaaahhh! Aaaaahhhh!*"

My mother came running down the stairs: "What's going on? A robbery?"

"No, Mom! What happened to the ketchup?"

She said, "Oh, it was a little low. You know, there was only a little ketchup left, so I just added a bit of water to make it last longer."

"You watered down my ketchup! You ruined my hamburger!" At this point, I pretended to start choking her—which she always thought was hysterical. "You ruined my hamburger!"

My father stumbled in and screamed, "WHAT THE HELL IS GOING ON HERE?"

"My hamburger! Your wife ruined my hamburger!"

Mom was still sputtering, "The ketchup—it was a little low . . ."

"But Ma! You save a dollar—while I spent twenty-two bucks to put this hamburger together! Now it's a puddle!"

I ate the burger, anyway. But, ooooooh, the *weeeeeste!*

■   ■   ■

Making my mother laugh was always a great source of pleasure to me. She was somewhat withdrawn, probably the effect of having had a horrible childhood back in Scotland—something I didn't learn until much later. Her parents divorced in an era when divorce was almost unknown. My understanding is that her mother ran off with another man—but this was never discussed much. That left her father with four children to care for, which was more than he could handle. Although it now sounds odd, in a Scottish house it was customary in those days to give away a child when there were too many of them. And that's what happened to my mom.

5

She told me a story about the time her dad brought her to a woman to see if the woman would temporarily take her in. This story is a wonderful example of how naive my mother was her whole life. Apparently, this woman lived at the seaport and, as my mom would tell it, "She was very nice to me, but I didn't want to stay. The funny thing was, this woman had lots of *uncles* and *brothers* who would come over every day! In fact, every day a different uncle or brother would come by and also bring me a gift."

The first time I heard this, I said, "Ma! I think that was a *brothel*! You lived in a brothel!"

"No!" she screamed. "It was nothing of the kind!"

"But you said it was by the docks?"

"Yes, yes."

"And every day different men would come over?"

"Yes."

"And they would give you a little gift and introduce themselves as an *uncle* or *brother*?"

"Ohhhhhhhhhhh . . . Oh! Maybe you're right . . ."

■   ■   ■

She was still a little girl when she left Scotland in 1923. Sixty years later, I took her back for the first time—along with my dad and my wife, Mavis. Mom was worried that things might not have changed since she left during the war. As she was packing for this return trip, she actually asked, "Should I bring toilet paper and soap?" I told her that we would probably be staying *indoors* at nice hotels.

So we were off to Glasgow, where she spent her childhood. For a time, she had worked as a servant girl in a big manor house. She would always tell me that part of her job there was to polish this enormous, long table that stood in the foyer of the manor. It would take her forever to do it. So I said, "Let's see if we can find that house." She wasn't convinced this was a good idea. She was still so ashamed of having been a servant girl. I said, "Ma, nobody cares about that!" I think she was afraid they'd hand her a rag and make her go polish the table again.

Anyway, Glasgow had changed, and she wasn't sure how to find the house. So I stopped a policeman who must have been seventy-five years old, and asked him for some directions. My mom said to him, "You know, I grew up here!" She told him what school she'd attended.

"Ach!" the policeman said. "I went to that school meself! When were you there?"

"Oh, 1919."

"Good heavens!" the cop said, recognizing her somewhat. "You look much older!"

The Scottish, I guess, have their own special way of appealing to a woman's vanity. My mother, in any case, thought it was very funny. Mavis might have killed the guy.

We finally found the big house, which had now been divided up into condominiums. So we rang the bell and got

Mavis and Dad with Mom on her first trip back to Scotland. Does my mom look happy or what?

into the main foyer—and the table was still there! My mother was amazed: "Oh, this is the table!" On the spot, I tried to buy it. I told her, "Ma, you're going to spend the rest of your life polishing this table at home!" She thought this was hysterical. Although she did look slightly relieved when the guy there said he wouldn't sell it for any price.

Next, we tried to find the site of the house where she was born. So we went to Captain's Road, where it had stood before being bombed during the war. Meanwhile, rain was pouring down and my father was hollering, "WHAT THE HELL ARE WE DOING OUT HERE IN THE GODDAMN RAIN!" And my mother was totally disoriented, wandering in circles, muttering, "I know it was here *somewhere* . . ." This went on for, oh, about forty-five minutes. Finally, she spotted some half-destroyed cement staircase that went nowhere and she stared and stared at it.

"Ma, do you think this is it?" I asked her.

"I think so."

I knew exactly how to get a rise out of her and saw this as the perfect moment. So I went over and grabbed her by the neck like I was choking her and started screaming: "THE MONEY! YOU CRAZY WOMAN! WHERE DID YOU BURY THE MONEY?! YOU SAID IT WAS HERE!" And my mother, who was seventy, just fell down in the street, laughing hysterically in the rain. Mom always had an odd sense of humor.

■ ■ ■

As an immigrant to this country, she lived in constant fear of breaking the law. Deportation, in her mind, was always just around the corner. I used to do a joke about this. I'd say that twice a month Mom checked the mattress tags, making sure they were on there good and tight. Just in case the police should come and inspect the bedding!

The truth is, although she was incredibly bright, my mother was always embarrassed about her level of education. I don't think it extended much beyond the third grade. She never told me. For that reason, she always stressed the importance of education to me—which was kind of sad, because I may have been the worst student in the history of academia. Probably the last written test Mom ever took was her American citizenship exam, which she passed only barely—under very funny circumstances. But, in her heart, she felt that she had failed and it would be only a matter of time before the immigration agents showed up.

The story, as I heard it, was that my father took her to the local immigration department, where the citizenship tests were given. You could miss up to four questions and still pass—and, on this day, Mom missed five. She flunked the test. And the question she flunked on was: "What is the Constitution of the United States?"

The answer my mother gave was: "A boat." Which wasn't entirely wrong: The USS *Constitution* was docked in Boston Harbor. But the judge instantly denied her citizenship, anyway. My father, of course, was outraged. He stormed up to the judge and started to argue.

"What the hell is this? Why did she fail? Let me see the test! She's not wrong—the *Constitution is* a boat! The woman got the question right! What the hell you doin'?"

The judge rolled his eyes and said, "No, the Constitution is our basic governing—"

"But it's also a boat in Boston! Am I wrong? Come on! It's a boat! She got it right!"

"Sir . . ."

"You ask her what it is—it's a ship down in Boston! The *Constitution*! Same thing! Come on!"

And the judge couldn't take any more. He just said, "Oh, for Christ's sake, *fine*! Here you go—give me the damn test! There! She's a *citizen*! Now just get out of here, sir!"

So my father showed my mom. "See that? You passed!"

"No, I didn't pass!" she whimpered. "They're going to come after me!"

"No, they're not gonna come after ya! The man said you passed!"

"But I got it wrong!"

"No, you didn't get it wrong!"

My mother worried about this until the day she died. Any time she was stopped for a traffic ticket or was even in the proximity of a policeman, she quaked with fear that they'd know about the Constitution question and how my dad had bullied the judge. When I took her to Scotland, she asked me, "Will I be able to get back in?"

"Ma! Don't worry! That was sixty years ago! They don't know that you said a boat!"

"Well, you know, sometimes just to get rid of you . . ."

"Ma, you're a citizen! Your passport says you're a citizen of the United States!"

"But they've got fancy lawyers who . . ."

It never ended.

■ ■ ■

He never directed it toward the family so much as at anyone else who might have provoked him. And he didn't let go of things easily. To this end, perhaps the defining incident of his life took place when he was about thirteen. This was in the Bronx during the Depression. He had been sent with a few dollars to buy groceries for his mother. He got as far as the corner when a gang of seven kids jumped him and took the money. Of course, my father was humiliated. Losing the money was the worst thing that could have ever happened. So he swore revenge.

Right away, he started going down to the gym to build up his muscles and to learn how to box. Eventually, he became a very tough amateur prizefighter. And that's when he decided it

The only time Dad didn't have his arm around Mom was when it was around me or Pat.

was time to find the seven guys who humiliated him. Over the course of the next few years, he managed to track down and punch the lights out of six of them. But he could never find the seventh guy. Apparently, he moved away or something. This drove my dad crazy. So much so that he never gave up searching. Never. To the point where—and I swear this is true—at age eighty-three, on his deathbed, he called me over close to him and said, "That seventh guy—that son of a bitch! I never found that guy!"

I guess that I inherited the same tenaciousness from him. Even though I'm not much of a fighter. I did, however, promise him that I'd try to find that Seventh Man. Of course, he'd have to be in his late nineties by now. I think I could probably take him.

■ ■ ■

My dad was an insurance man for most of his life. It was a perfect fit for him. He was always very gregarious, a good people guy and a great salesman. Before this, he had worked such jobs as turning over bottles at a Coca-Cola factory and driving a truck. Then his oldest brother, John, got him hired at Prudential Insurance, where my dad worked until he retired. Uncle John was the only Leno at that point to have gone to college—a privilege given to the oldest boy in most immigrant families. His degree got him the Prudential job, and right away, he knew that my dad had the ideal street smarts to push policies door-to-door. So when my dad started there, he asked, "What's the toughest area?" The other salesmen said, "Harlem, Spanish Harlem. Those people don't care about insurance!" But my dad said, "Oh, no? I'll go up there!"

Although he never had any trouble, he would tell funny stories about how the big thing in Harlem at that time was to rob the insurance man. Robbers would always take the insurance guy's pants or clothes, so he wouldn't run through the streets, yelling for police. (At conventions, unfailingly, there would be jokes about the five naked insurance guys stuck in the Harlem stairwell.) But my dad always liked working in Harlem. For a street guy, he was never, ever, heard to utter an ethnic or racial slur. He hated any type of prejudice. In fact, not long ago, I got a letter from a woman who wanted to know if my dad might have been the same "Mr. Leeno" who would come around every week to collect a nickel from her family. (Nickel policies were common for people who didn't have big incomes.) Apparently, he always brought candy for the children and would often be invited in for dinner. This woman remembered waiting for him every week and said he was really the first white person she ever knew.

Eventually, he worked his way up the ranks and became the Andover office manager, where he won all kinds of sales awards for his division. Because he was a very funny guy, he was often asked to get up and speak at insurance conventions. I remember seeing him working on jokes, writing them out on big yellow pads. I was always fascinated to see where he'd cross out certain phrases, depending on what the audience would be like. If there were religious people present, for instance, he'd change lines like ". . . and they ran like hell" to "ran like blazes!" And if he was accepting some accolade, he would always use me in his speech and say, "My boy just said, 'They can't mean you, Dad!'" This was just mortifying to me. Afterward, I'd say to him, "I never said that!" And he'd laugh.

15

Years later, when I began telling stories about him on tele-vision, he'd call me and complain, *"Hey, I never said that!"* And I'd just tell him, "Well, you used to do it to me!" And I'd laugh.

■ ■ ■

By the time he retired, Dad was the last of the old breed of insurance men. Certainly, he was one of the last of the guys who'd risen in the company without the benefit of formal edu-cation. All of those great Italian street salesmen were long gone—but he had always kept up with the ongoing changes in the industry. There were moments, though, that the new breed of insurance punks gave him grief. And my dad could only take so much grief. I remember when he was about sixty-three, he came home from work and complained about one particular union guy who would come by his office and behave obnox-iously. This union guy couldn't have been much more than thirty, but he did a lot of unnecessary finger-pointing and hol-lering. Just a jerk. My dad couldn't stand him. He would say, "Oh, this guy is so annoying! What a son of a bitch!" Finally, the old prizefighter inside him couldn't take any more and he announced to us, "I'm gonna fight that guy!"

So, at the age of sixty-three, he started training! He'd go running every day, then work out with his speed bag. After about a month, the union guy showed up again. My father invited him into his office, where the guy launched into his yelling routine. My dad started to holler back, then suddenly: BOOM! My dad unloaded a punch and broke the guy's nose. Like any bully, the union guy said, "You son of a bitch! I'm get-tin' the cops!" And he ran out of the building.

At this point, my father pulled out his extra-thick eyeglasses and put in both of the big hearing aids he sometimes wore. Then he sat down at his desk and waited. The union guy returned with an Andover policeman, who asked, "What happened here, Mr. Leno? Did you beat up this man?"

My father squinted through his glasses, turned a hearing aid toward the cop, and innocently said, "What? I'm retired in two years! Why the hell am I going to fight a guy half my age? No, this guy slipped on the floor. I saw him fall down on his face."

The union guy was fuming. "I didn't fall on my face! This guy beat me up!"

The cop took a long look at both of them, then asked the union guy, "How old are you, son? Thirty?" He said thirty-three. Then the cop started laughing at him. This just infuriated the guy, who turned and stormed out of the office. My dad and the cop just kept on laughing.

2

BOILING TUCK

There were two things that were true about my childhood—I loved to make trouble and more than that I loved getting a reaction. Of course, I'm not sure how much my parents enjoyed it, but I was a kid—what did I know?

It probably all started innocently enough when I was about four. We were living in New Rochelle, New York, and I was in somebody's apartment surrounded by women—always an ideal situation! There was my mom, my Aunt Faye, my Aunt Edie, and some other women, and I was the center of attention, which I already knew was the greatest place to be. The women would always fawn over the children in the family and make us feel ridiculously special. Nowadays I guess you'd call that a support group. I was born with a head of curly hair, and all I ever heard was "Oh, look at the curls! He's the most handsome baby!" I actually used to think, "Hey, I'm the handsomest baby ever!" It wasn't until I was in my twenties and saw some pictures that it occurred to me that they might have been lying.

This was as cute as I ever got.

Anyway, that day I asked a question that weighed heavily on my mind. I pointed to my Aunt Faye's blouse and asked, "How come girls have humps like camels?" Suddenly, everyone was screaming like the room was on fire. "Ohhhhh! Did you hear what the child said?!!" Of course, my mother was red-faced. And the other women started having coughing spasms. And I thought, "What did I do?" I remember being amazed at the reaction and kind of liking how that felt.

The funny thing is, nobody ever answered the question.

■ ■ ■

I was never much interested in kids my own age. I always liked to listen to what the adults had to say because they always seemed much more interesting. One night in New Rochelle, my parents were having what I thought was a huge party, but I guess it was just two other couples over playing bridge. I had gone up to bed, but I'd crept back to the top of the stairs to eavesdrop on the party below. They were talking and laughing and having a good time, and I wanted so badly to be down there where the action was. So I hatched a plan: I would make a big showbiz entrance! I would slide down the banister in my pajamas, hit the bottom, land on my feet, and go, "*Ta daaaa!*" Right in the middle of the bridge game! I'd be the life of the party! Cause a sensation! Be like Liza Minnelli—who, of course, would have been about eight at the time, but still no doubt a load of excitement.

So I balanced myself on the top of the banister and slid approximately one inch. And that was it. Suddenly, I fell like a nuclear missile—straight through a table with a lamp on it. There was a huge crash as the table collapsed and the lamp shattered. Everybody jumped up from the card game, scared out of their minds. But what an entrance! My parents rushed me to the hospital, where my spleen had to be removed. Which was so cool to me at the time—well worth giving up an insignificant body part. I've never really missed my spleen, anyway.

■ ■ ■

As you can probably tell from the burger story earlier, I have a deep love for meat, and it began early. My parents instilled it in me. Having lived through the Depression, they thrilled to the idea of meat, like it was gold. My father would often tell the story of the Italian guy who wrote home to the old country and bragged that he ate meat *twice a week*. Somebody said to him, "But you're eating meat *every day*!" And the Italian guy said, "Yeah, but they'd never believe it."

Anyway, other kids lived for chocolate. Not me. I wanted

meat and would do anything to get it! Like the time when I was six and my father decided to build a flagstone patio behind our house at 69 Leland Avenue in New Rochelle. This was going to be barbecue heaven! When the patio was finished, Dad was so proud that he wanted to celebrate. This, of course, was appalling to my mom, who believed you should never talk about your accomplishments. But my dad couldn't be suppressed. He'd drag everybody out to the patio and crow, "Hey, I built this myself!" So he announced, "Let's have all the relatives over and show this off!"

Meanwhile, we had just gotten one of those GE rotisseries, the kind with the motorized spit that rotates the meat for hours. My mom bought a huge five-pound roast beef for the party, tied it up with string, and put it on the spit. Everyone came over and they were inside the house talking while the roast beef was out turning on the patio. And, for me,

Me on the famous patio, with Bruce, the roast-beef-eating dog!

this spinning meat was just an amazing spectacle. Juice was dripping. Fat was sizzling brown. The spit was making little *eeee-eeee-eeee* noises as it turned. I couldn't take my eyes off it. And I was dying to taste it. But I couldn't reach up high enough to get at it.

Then I got an idea: I pulled out my trusty plastic Ace pocket comb, which was just long enough to reach the meat. I stuck it into the turning roast, got a little juice, then licked it off the comb. (Okay, so I was a weird kid.) Worked perfectly. I did it over and over again. "This is great," I thought. And then the worst happened: The comb got caught in the meat string! I couldn't pull it loose because the roast kept turning. I let go and now the comb was stuck spinning on the meat—and it's slowly melting! I didn't know what to do. So I left it and tip-toed away.

After an hour or so, it was time to bring the roast beef inside. By now, my dad couldn't be more excited. We all sat down and he was bursting with pride: "Oh boy! A new patio! It's a beautiful day! And, hey! Take a look at that roast beef!" So he started to carve the roast beef with a big knife. He tried to cut off a little slice and, all of a sudden, he was struggling with the knife. It sounded like he was sawing wood. Then a big chunk of plastic fell on the plate and went *clank!* The meat was all pink underneath. My dad started breathing hard, like he was going to explode.

He said, "What the hell is this?!"

So, very quietly, I said, "Oh . . . um . . . it's my comb. I guess it, uh, melted on the roast beef . . ."

"WHAT!? What are you talking about? How the hell does a comb melt on roast beef! Do you know how much that roast beef cost! Give me that goddamn thing!"

With that, he picked up the roast like a football and threw it out in the yard. Our dog, Bruce, as well as the other neighborhood dogs smelled it and, within seconds, started ripping it to shreds. And, of course, everybody was just sitting there at the table, mouths hanging open, stunned! The meat had been totally devoured by dogs. I'd never seen my dad so angry. He screamed at me, "Now I'm going to put *you* on the rotisserie!" And my mom was saying, "Oh, don't be so hard on the boy." I slunk off, feeling stupid and very hungry.

One thing occurs to me now: That was the first time in my life that I was really jealous of a dog.

■ ■ ■

As a kid, I never did anything unless somebody was watching. Even now, that's probably still true. You can't be funny all by yourself. I've tried it in front of a mirror and—*nothing*! You just can't tell jokes in a vacuum. I tried that once, too, but you wouldn't believe the dust. So I learned to be kind of a show-off. But I always wondered why I behaved the way I did. Then I read a book called *Mike Mulligan and His Steam Shovel*, which made a huge impression on me. For some reason, I read it in the coal cellar of our next-door neighbors, the Vollens, while sitting on top of their coal heap. This probably made a huge impression on my pants, which must have pleased my mom.

There was one line in the book that fascinated me because it really sort of summed up everything about my life until that point—and until this point, too. The old steam shovel, named Mary Anne, is busy digging a hole where a skyscraper will be built, and a crowd starts to gather. The book said, "When people used to stop and watch them, Mike Mulligan and Mary

Anne used to dig a little faster and a little better. The more people stopped, the faster and better they dug." As if the machine was somehow drawing power from the people around it. And that made sense to me, a perfectly logical reason to dig a great hole or act like an idiot in public. (The only problem—which I blame on my hopelessly gnatlike attention span—is that I never finished reading the book. In the end, Mike and the shovel dug such a great hole that they never got out. I can relate to that, too.)

When I was about seven, other kids thought it was cool to tape baseball cards to their bicycle spokes so the bikes would sound like motorcycles. I wanted to improve on the idea and amaze my friends. Besides, I didn't have any baseball cards. I thought I could do something flashier. So I went to the little grocery store in New Rochelle to look for picture magazines. My eyes fell on the perfect solution: girlie magazines! They obviously didn't sell *Playboy* or *Penthouse*, but they did have things like *Argosy* and *True Men's Adventure* and *Nugget*, with fascinating confessional stories like "I Was Castro's Harlot." There'd be cheesy illustrations of allegedly sexy scenes—things like two men grabbing a woman as a bullet glances off one of her bra straps, causing it to fall down. Just horribly embarrassing stuff. I bought a bunch of these magazines, went home, cut out all the pictures, and pasted them on my bike. Now I'd be like Hugh Hefner on a two-wheeler!

Naturally, I couldn't wait to ride around the neighborhood and impress other second-graders. So I pedaled down the sidewalk and parked the bike at a friend's house, where a crowd started to gather. I was swaggering with importance! Then my friend's mother came out to see what the commotion was. She took one look at the bike and went back inside. Thirty seconds later, I heard a car screeching around the corner.

My dad.

In his '57 Plymouth.

He slammed into the driveway, picked up the bike, threw it in the trunk, and peeled off. I walked home that day. I think I told the kids it was a factory recall.

■ ■ ■

I was in the fourth grade when I told what seemed like my first real adult joke. We had just moved to Andover, Massachusetts—and, up until then, if I was funny, it was only because I did stupid, obnoxious things. But this was different. I was in Mrs. Allen's class and we were studying the legends of Robin Hood. Mrs. Allen was telling us how cruel the Sheriff of Nottingham was and how Robin's merry men were often captured, then boiled in oil. I raised my hand with what I thought was an insightful observation.

I said, "They couldn't boil Tuck!"

Mrs. Allen said, "Why not?"

"Because he was a friar!"

(What do you want—I was *nine!*)

The class laughed and Mrs. Allen smiled just a little. Then she said, "All right, enough of that! Quiet down!" But seeing her smile was such a triumph—vastly preferable to being sent to the principal's office, which was the usual response. Then, for the next couple of days, other teachers would ask me, "What was it you said in Mrs. Allen's class?" Apparently, she had tried to relay it in the teachers' lounge and screwed it up. And I thought, "Geez, I like this!" I hadn't felt that kind of

I still can't knot a tie correctly.

power before. All because I said something that was actually funny. Eventually, I even got to tell the principal—as soon as I did something stupid again, which didn't take long.

▪ ▪ ▪

I'll admit it: I have a big head. It's just large. Always was. Other kids were fascinated with my head. Not so much with its lack of content, but with its actual size. My alleged friend George Moss used to tease me about it. He was convinced that it was impervious to pain. He'd say, "Hey, Jay, you've got a hard head there!" Sounded good to me. One day, when we were nine, he decided to test it. He pulled out a hammer. "Why don't we see if this hurts?" he said. Right away, other kids seconded the motion. I wasn't thrilled with the idea, but I figured I'd play along for laughs. So I bent down and George swung the hammer and hit me on the head.

Bonk!

Let me say now—this was the sort of searing pain where you're just fighting back the tears stinging behind your eyes. But, like a moron, I said, "Ha ha ha! It didn't hurt at all!" The kids were amazed! So George did it again, even harder this time.

BONK!

Agony. I winced and said, "Not a thing!"

And George hit me again.

BONNNKKK!!!!

This time I think I actually said, "*Ouch!!!*"

But I smiled anyway, then suggested we do something else that didn't involve bludgeoning. Besides, there were birds circling my head that needed to be chased. If there's a moral here—and I doubt there is—it was the realization that I would do anything to get a laugh, including invite friends to fracture my skull. Playing out the moment was better than any possible pain. Although I do remember hiding in my room the day I saw George walking around the neighborhood with a mallet and chisel.

■ ■ ■

Andover was a wonderful place to grow up—just an ideal American town that never lost its innocence. People got excited over the littlest things. Your best friend would call up with incredible news like "Oh, man, one of those new Corvettes just drove by!" And you'd be devastated—screaming "*No! No!*"—because you missed this cataclysmic event. But it was a magical town with everything a kid would want—a waterfall, creeks, a pond, a swimming hole, an old mill, a haunted house. There was even an actual ghost town from the 1800s—knocked down storefronts and an old saloon—where you could find arrowheads and Indian artifacts. And then there was the town ice cream parlor, which, ironically enough, was run by the meanest man in town.

My friends and I just hated this guy—an awful fat guy who had a Cadillac that he treated like his baby. And he also had a police dog, a Doberman with the same terrible disposition as its owner, and he'd usually leave the dog inside the Cadillac. But sometimes the dog would be unleashed, and invariably it would growl and chase us into the parking lot, where we'd drop our ice cream cones as we fled. The dog was just psychotic. I remember one day when we were hanging around in front of the ice cream parlor. The guy, as usual, came outside and hollered, "Hey, you kids! Don't get near that Cadillac! Keep away from that Cadillac! It's a very expensive car!" This, of course, only made us want to go near it. So we went over to the Cadillac, where the dog was in the backseat, growling at us.

"RRRrrrrrr!"

For fun, my friend started to bang on the roof of the car. And the dog went nuts.

"RRRrrrrrrr! RRRRRrrrrr!"

It couldn't get at us through the windows, so out of frustration, the dog began to rip up the dashboard with its teeth! We thought that was hysterical. So we went around, banging on all the fenders. Inside the car, the dog was now spinning around, biting off chunks of the upholstery.

"RRRRRrrrrrrrrRRRRRRRRRrrrrrrRRRRRRRR!"

And, of course, we're screaming and laughing, like it was the funniest thing we'd ever seen. The interior was in shreds!

Then we innocently slunk back to eat our ice cream cones when the guy finally came outside. He took one look at the car and began screaming at the dog! What we'd done was terrible, of course, but it nevertheless felt like we'd triumphed for the good of mankind, if not dogkind.

■   ■   ■

Always looking to keep me occupied in some constructive way, my parents had given me a dorky rubber stamp kit—with stamps like TOP SECRET! and CONFIDENTIAL! and one that you could use to design your own. For whatever reason, I especially prized the TOP SECRET! stamp. I don't know what made me do this, but I addressed an envelope to the FBI, Washington, D.C., and stamped it TOP SECRET! Then for the return address I wrote *Leno* and our home address. But I left off any postage. Just to see what would happen, I went down to the Andover post office, threw the envelope on the floor, and ran like hell.

So that night we were sitting at dinner and the doorbell rang. My dad opened the door and there stood a man looking very nervous. He said, "Mr. Leno, I'm the postmaster here in Andover." At this point, I began worrying about how many years I'd be doing in the Big House. We had moved to town only the year before and didn't really know most people. And most of them didn't know us, either. Now we were about to become known as Spy Family Leno.

So the postmaster said, "It's none of my business, sir, but did you drop some, er, *documents* at the post office today?"

My father hadn't a clue. "Uh, no."

The postmaster's eyes lit up. "*Oh!* Don't worry—I understand, Mr. Leno! Believe me, it doesn't go any further than this!"

My father, stymied, said, "What are you talking about?"

And the postmaster winked at him and laughed. "Ho ho ho! I just want to return this to you. Normally, we'd return it by mail, but I felt because of the stamp and the addressee that I would bring it over myself."

My father took the envelope, saw FBI, Washington, his name in the corner, TOP SECRET!—and said, "Oh! All right! Thank you very much!"

The postmaster told him, "Any other problems, Mr. Leno, you come talk directly to me. Anytime you need something mailed special. Not a word about this."

He left and my father had no idea what was going on. Then he looked at me. Big trouble coming. He said, "What is this all about?" So I told him. He was furious! He took the stamp kit and crunched it up. But there was a happy ending, after all.

From that day forward, every time he went down to the post office, the postmaster would give him a wink and say, "Oh, come to the front of the line, Mr. Leno! No problem. How's business in Washington?"

And my father would wink back and say, "Oh, fine, fine! Just broke up a big spy ring in Wilmington over the weekend!"

■ ■ ■

My father always tried to get me to do outdoorsy things. He'd say, "Why don't you go fishing or something?"

"I hate fishing, Pop."

Fishing, to me, was like a nap with a stick. But he wouldn't hear of it. So he bought me a fishing rod and reel. My mother said to me, "Go fishing one time. Your father wants to see you do things like that."

"But I hate fishing!"

"Just go fishing," she said. "If you catch one fish, you can at least show your father that you used the fishing rod."

The idea made me sick. Then one day at school I heard some kids talk about catching a lot of fish. I said, "Where's a lot of fish?" They said, "They're draining this lake near our house and there are all these fish there!" I figured that if the lake is drained, fish have got to be flipping around everywhere. How hard could this be?

So I rode my bike over and found all these dead fish at the bottom of the lake. I scooped up about twenty-five fish and brought them home. I walked in and said, "Hey, Pop! Look what I caught today!"

My father just beamed with pride. "Hey! Look at my boy! Look at all the fish he got there! I knew you could do it!"

My mother looked at me sideways. "*Well!* You certainly caught a lot of fish!"

"Oh, yeah, Ma. It was easy!"

So my mother decided to fry them up. She cut them open and started gagging from the smell! She sliced into about six before saying, "All these fish stink! Jamie, where'd you get these fish? We can't eat these!"

My dad said, "Oh, I'm sure they're fine! What a little fisherman!"

My mother finally took me aside and gave me one of those looks. So I confessed under threat of frying pan: "Okay, okay— *I found 'em!* They've been dead for days!" My mom was exasperated, but so as not to disappoint my dad, she ran out to the store and bought fresh fish, which she served that night. Dad never found out. He did wonder, though, why I gave up my fishing career on such an impressive note.

▪ ▪ ▪

Then my dad decided to install a basketball backboard on a wooden pole in the driveway. This was another terrible idea. Getting sweaty from throwing a ball through a net! I said, "Dad, I don't want a basketball net. I hate basketball."

My dad said, "The other kids play! I want you to play basketball, too!"

So we dug a hole, poured cement, and put up a huge backboard. I hated this thing. Loathed it. Every day he'd come home from the office and say, "Come on, we'll play a little basketball!" I'd groan, "Pop, I hate basketball." Never mind that! He'd insist we take a few shots—until I'd feign some pathetic injury like a broken fingernail or a stubbed toe. Meanwhile, I had an

The only time I would ever be photographed in uniform.

algebra tutor named Mr. Murphy, who'd come over after school. One day he was trying to back his car up the driveway—and I saw my opportunity to end the merciless basketball torture! Mr. Murphy couldn't quite see through his rearview mirror, so I helped "guide" him. I said, "Come on back! You're okay! Back farther, Mr. Murphy! Back back back back!" And he followed instructions perfectly!

CRAAAAAACCKKKK!

Right into the backboard. The wooden pole snapped! The hoop was down! Mr. Murphy was so embarrassed: "Oh, I broke the backboard! I'm so sorry!" (I could barely mask my glee.) That night my father got home and screamed, "WHAT THE HELL HAPPENED HERE?" I said, "Um, Mr. Murphy . . . had a little accident." My father felt awful. "Oh, Mr. Murphy . . . oh Jesus, that's too bad. He's a nice man, that Mr. Murphy."

"Yeah, Pop, very nice man."

Free at last! And the backboard never returned. We didn't want to remind Mr. Murphy of his humiliation. Very nice man.

■ ■ ■

But my father never gave up. Inevitably, he tried this one: "Why don't you join the Boy Scouts!" Now, I never liked joining groups, and this one, in particular, worried me because you were required to attend meetings wearing uniforms with shorts. And, worse still, a neckerchief! I couldn't have looked dorkier. Certainly, the Boy Scouts are a wonderful organization—if you like belonging to organizations. But playing with rope? Fun with wood? Not for me, thank you. And yet, for one brief hellish moment, I became a morose and reluctant Scout.

I hated all the regimentation. One day, our scoutmaster announced, "I want your parents to get involved." I figured, "Great! Let Dad get a taste of this nightmare!" So he called my father, who tried to squirm out of it. "I don't have time for the Boy Scouts!" he said. "I got a new patio to build here!"

The scoutmaster wouldn't let up. "No, you *have* to get involved for the sake of the boys! I want you to give out merit badges. If you parents don't give out the merit badges and give the tests, how will the kids understand their accomplishments! I mean, *I can't do everything here!*"

This was a very high-strung guy.

So he brought over a bunch of merit badges for my dad to award us. That day my father took our whole troop out into the backyard and concocted a quick way to get rid of the badges. He said, "Come on out here, kids! Now tell me—what kind of tree is that?" He pointed to an apple tree. Duh.

"*It's an apple tree!*" we all shouted.

"How can you tell?" he asked. Duh.

"*It's got apples on it!*"

"Okay! Very good! Here you go, kids!"

And he proceeded to hand out all the merit badges—like six badges per kid. Badges for accomplishments in fishing, in corn-raising, in woodcarving—everything I couldn't do if my life depended on it. All of them now earned in one fell swoop for recognizing apples. This was great! So we all proudly went back to Scout headquarters, where our scoutmaster looked like he was about to have a heart attack. He started running around grabbing away our new badges. "Give me that!" he's shouting, and ripping at our uniforms. Kids are crying and kicking him.

Finally, he got my father on the phone and started yelling

at him: "Are you nuts? You can't give away badges for identify-ing apple trees!"

"Why not! They knew the right answer!"

They kept on yelling at each other for an hour. And that was pretty much the end of my Boy Scout tour. Later, my father said, "Why the hell would you want to belong to that kind of organization, anyway? They're all nuts!"

■ ■ ■

Football was the final frontier—of my hopeless ineptitude. I was always big for my age, but the opposite of athletic. That didn't matter. At that time, in a town like Andover, boys played football and girls took home ec. I would have rather taken home ec, just to be near girls. Not to mention, the food they burned. (Burned meat is still meat!) But in fifth and sixth grades, I played peewee football—which sounds like an embar-rassment in itself. Which it was. By eighth grade, at Andover South Junior High, I played left tackle very badly.

I don't know why I played. I had no interest in football. Worse yet, we had to study *playbooks*, which was cruel and unusual punishment. It was homework! I could barely do homework for school, and when I did, it needed to be decoded before it was graded F. Why would I want to do it for a stupid game? And so I never did.

Finally—and, in my case, I do mean *finally*—there came the day of the Big Game with our bitter rival, North Andover. For what seemed like *hundreds* of years, the North and South schools *hated* each other. And, each year, this particular game might as well have been the Super Bowl. People from both sides of town would show up and just spit at each other! I've never been able to run that kind of emotional gamut with regard to sports. I can barely run an emotional gamut with regard to life. In fact, I can barely *run*. Which, of course, made me a remarkable left tackle.

By halftime that day, we were losing—and that's when the coach launched into his big pep talk. He wanted to rile us up, so that we'd go back out there bloodthirsty for the North team. "Ridiculous," I thought. "It's just football!" But he acted like the fate of all humanity hung in the balance. So he tried this stupid tactic:

"I wanna tell you boys a little something," he started, with a terribly dramatic tone. "Ordinarily, I wouldn't tell you this— but you're MEN!" (*We're boys? We're men? We're TWELVE, for God's sake—what an idiot!*) He went on: "I'm gonna tell you about a little incident that happened last week when I was in North Andover—"

Already, the other players were *aghast*: "Hey, what were you doin' over there!?" This was an outrage! Like he'd gone to the Mekong Delta or over to the wrong side in Nam.

"Never mind that!" the coach said. "I'm walkin' down Main Street behind a coupla wise guys from North. I guess they didn't know WHO I AM—hard to believe! And I heard them talkin' about . . . our team!"

By now, everybody was hanging on his every obviously phony word.

"What'd they say? What'd they say?"

"Well," the coach said, "I normally don't repeat this kind of *gutter talk*. There's no place for it on this team—but I heard one of them say that our team was a bunch of . . . ASS-HOLES!!!"

The rest of the team grit their teeth and recoiled! "*Oohhhhhhhhh!*"

But I just burst out laughing. "HA HA HA HA! Oh, *come on! THAT NEVER HAPPENED! HA HA!*"

I quickly realized that this was the wrong response. The other players glared at me. And the coach's face was flushed and full of rage!

"LENO!" he screamed. "WHY DON'T YOU JUST GET THE HELL OUTTA HERE!"

I said, "What did I do?"

"GET OUT! JUST GET THE HELL OFF THIS TEAM! THERE'S NO PLACE HERE FOR PEOPLE LIKE YOU!"

And so I got kicked off the team that day, thus ending my gridiron career—and probably changing the course of American football. I hope so, anyway.

■　■　■

Girls were easiest to make laugh. But they were even easier to annoy. I was always good at that. For instance, I loved to torment Debbie and Candy Maher, two sisters who lived up the street. I would regularly climb on top of their house at night while they were asleep, sneak into their bedroom window, tie all their underwear in knots, then slip back out. At that age, I had no idea what else to do with underwear. One time, their father came home late, saw me on the roof, and thought I was a burglar. I jumped down and ran into the woods before the police came. I was scared to death! That night, I didn't know what to do with *my* underwear.

■　■　■

A few years later, when I was about twelve or thirteen, my parents decided it was time for me to hear about the Facts of Life. And because they were old-fashioned parents, this was the most dreaded task in all of child-raising. They used to bicker over it. Occasionally, I would hear my mother say to my father, "You've got to talk to the boy and explain some things!"

And my dad would say, "What the hell kind of things does he need to know!"

"Will you just have a talk with him!"

Finally, when they couldn't put it off any longer, my mother one day deliberately left the house, so that this father-son rite of passage could take place. My father called me out of my room and said, "Come in here! Your mother wants me to talk to you a little about the birds and the bees. You know anything about this birds and bees nonsense?"

I shrugged and said, "Well, yeah, Dad, I guess I know a little bit."

"GOOD, GOOD! HOW DO THE RED SOX LOOK THIS YEAR? YOU THINK THEY'LL GO ALL THE WAY? WHAT DO YOU THINK?"

And that was pretty much my formal education about sex.

3

MOM, BY A TKO

When it came to vacations, my father and I were exactly alike. We didn't want to go. I'll never forget one summer when my mother forced me to go to Scout camp. "Oh, you'll love it!" she said. "You'll be with all the other boys!" I told her, "I don't want to bond with boys!" But they sent me anyway. I hated it! Every second of every day there, I'd think, "Why am I here? What am I doing?" And I would write pleading letters home: "What did I do wrong? I'll never do it again!" There was no amount of groveling I wouldn't do to get out of that kind of torture.

To this day, I can't take a vacation. I'd rather hang around the house and get things done. My dad was the same way. But even he had to cave in once in a while. For Mom. One summer, she announced, "I think we should take a family vacation. Let's rent a boat and go up to Newfound Lake in New Hampshire for a week." My father protested: "Why? We've got a beautiful home right here! And a *week*!" But there was no way out.

On the long car trip there, all I did was whine and complain, as all kids do. And my father, as all fathers do, said, "Hey! Cut it out or I'll turn this car around right now! We'll go right back home!" This was when I could feel my power. I said, "Go ahead, Dad. We're two states from home—a thousand miles away! Teach me a lesson! Cancel the reservations. Lose your deposit. Go ahead, Pop. I dare you!" Hey, at least I tried.

But it didn't help. We were trapped in a stupid cabin on a lake with a boat. My dad and I were miserable. One day, out on the boat, I said to him, "What are we doin', Pop?" And he put up the good front and said, "Your mother wants this! This is for your mother!" But he was hating it. We sat floating for a few minutes. Then I said, "Maybe if something happened to the boat . . ." His eyes lit up a little bit. Suddenly, he raced the boat toward a jutting rock, which cracked the wooden hull. Water came flowing in. We were thrilled. Mom was terrified. The vacation lasted only three days. We got home with plenty of time to do yardwork.

▪ ▪ ▪

Probably wisely, my parents never liked to acknowledge anything that ever happened after the 1950s. This seemed to make all of my own points of reference a little antiquated. For instance, whereas other kids had refrigerators in their homes, we had an *ice box*. Same machine—different epoch of the twentieth century!

Even our record player was known as the Victrola—long after actual Victrolas were extinct. In fact, *any* kind of stereo was a Victrola. For example, when I was in high school, I went out and got myself one of those quadraphonic four-speaker stereos. I brought it home and started setting it up—when my father stuck his head into my room. "*Heeeeey!*" he said. "Whaddya got there—a new Victrola?" I said, "Yeah, Pop, it's a new Victrola! Could ya wind it up for me? The handle's right there on the side!"

Naturally, then, my introduction to the Beatles came through our "Victrola"—which would have been difficult to explain to John Lennon. I remember when the Beatles first appeared on the *Ed Sullivan Show*. I was in the eighth grade, feeling the onset of that inevitable teenage rebellion. I ran through the house and said, "Oh, we gotta watch these guys, Dad!" So we turned on our old black-and-white TV—the kind that made loud *caa-chonnkk* noises every time you changed the channel. The Beatles started to sing, but I noticed that my father was reading his newspaper, paying no attention at all. And I thought, "Why isn't my father watching the most important event of the twentieth century?"

So I tried to get him interested. I said, "You know, Dad, they write all their own music!"

And my father put the paper down, heaved a big sigh, and said, "Let me tell you something—some manager gives these kids a couple of bucks to go out there and act loony and you all go nuts and fall for it!"

Oh, I see, that's really all it takes to be the biggest commercial success in the history of music! This was so ridiculous to me.

And that's probably why I never fought with my parents. It was just such an obvious generation gap, all I could do was laugh. And then, of course, go put another Beatles record on the Victrola.

▪ ▪ ▪

Our family once had a Ford Galaxie 500. Nice enough car, but not very interesting. Boring, in fact. It had rubber floor mats and thick vinyl upholstery, which meant you could hose it off with all four doors open, inside and out. (Smelled great afterward, if you don't mind mildew.) Inevitably, the time came to get a new car. So I said, "Dad, can't we get something a little fancier this time?" Dad wasn't so sure. But my mother said, "Oh, let the boy help you!"

So we headed up to Shawsheen Motors in Andover to find the next car. We decided, of course, on the new '66 Galaxie 500, but I piped up and asked, "Dad, can I help pick the engine?" He grumbled a bit. Mom said, "Oh, let the boy pick the engine! What difference does it make?" So my dad shrugged and took my mom off to look at Ford Falcons. I sat down with the dealer and impressed him with my knowledge of cars. I said, "This is what we want: We want the Galaxie's Police Pursuit Package. The 428-cubic-inch engine, 360 horsepower with the 354 rear end and the muffler-delete option package." I was basically ordering a Highway Patrol car!

My dad came back and looked over the order. "What do you want with a 360-horsepower?"

I said, "Well, we live on a hill, Dad."

My mom sighed and said, "Oh, let the boy decide how much horsepower we need! What's the difference?"

My dad just shook his head and signed all the paperwork. About eight weeks later, we went down to pick up the car. Right away, my dad noticed that the car had the deep-dish inset wheels. He hollered, "There's no hubcaps! There's no hubcaps!"

"That's right, Mr. Leno," said the salesman. "You ordered it without hubcaps. That's part of the Police Pursuit Package."

"*What Police Pursuit Package?* Oh, all right!"

He got into the car, turned the key, and the engine revved like thunder, like a Boeing aircraft! Scared to death, my father screamed, "Aaaaaaaggghhhh! There's a hole in the muffler! There's a hole in the muffler!"

The sales guy ran back over and said, "No, no, Mr. Leno— you signed up for the muffler-delete option package!"

So now my father was just livid! He said, "I'm gettin' the hell outta here!" He put the car in gear and just barely touched the gas pedal—*SCREEEEEEEEEECHHH!* We exploded out of the car lot, smoke pouring out of the tires. We drove home like a rocket ship. You could hear it coming from blocks away, as it broke the sound barrier. We got home and my mom was aghast, just hated the car. My dad screamed and screamed at me.

But about two months later, I wandered into my dad's room, looking for something on his dresser. And there I saw a speeding ticket he had gotten for going one hundred ten miles per hour! So I guess he got used to the car.

■　■　■

Not all that coincidentally, my first real job the summer before high school was lot boy at Wilmington Ford. I always liked cars, especially Fords. I thought it would be fun to see how they came in from the factory. The father of one of my friends owned the dealership, and he hired me to do odd jobs to make the cars look presentable. I'd wash them as soon as they rolled off the trailers. Wilmington had an enormous lot—*literally acres of new Fords!*—and sometimes I would drive customers around on a golf cart to help them find certain cars.

Once, I was told to take a married couple to find a blue Ford at the far end of the lot. We got to the car and found one of the salesmen masturbating in the front seat! The woman looked in the car and shrieked, "*Aaaaaiiieeeeee!*" The salesman jumped out, pulled up his pants, and ran off to get fired. Fortunately, I didn't have to clean that car.

Another part of the job was to go out every morning and attach seventy sets of hubcaps. Then, at night, I'd take all of them off again to prevent kids from stealing them. One night, I was walking back to the building, carefully carrying a big wobbly pile of maybe thirty hubcaps. I went around a corner and saw this new hotshot sales manager, who made me kind of nervous. Suddenly, I lost hold of the hubcaps and they fell to the ground. None of them were dented, but there were some minor scratches. The new sales boss just tore into me.

"This is the Ford Motor Company," he hollered. "You can't treat our property this way! You're fired! Get out! Get out! I can't have you doing this to our merchandise!"

"I-I didn't mean it," I stammered. But he just fired me on the spot. I was so ashamed, I didn't even tell my parents. I acted like a forty-five-year-old guy who got canned. I'd kill time all day, hiding in a garage or at a friend's house, then go home at the usual hour. Mom would ask, "How was work today?" I'd say, "Oh, good, Ma!" It was horrible, but I didn't want them to know the shame of how I lost my first real job.

Then it occurred to me to appeal to the top guy. So I wrote a letter to Henry Ford II in Detroit. I explained how much I liked Fords and that my mom drove a Falcon and I made my dad buy a '66 Galaxie (I didn't mention the Police Pursuit Package) and that our next car would be another Ford. I told him that I hoped to one day buy a Ford of my own and that, in the meantime, I had been working at Wilmington Ford, but got fired just because I dropped some hubcaps. So I mailed it and waited to see what would happen.

The next thing I knew, I got a call from my old boss. He said, "I don't know who the hell you know in Detroit, but if you want your old job back, come on back here!" So I went back to work, which made the guy who fired me very nervous. He seemed to stay clear of me. Because now everyone knew that when I talked, Hank "The Deuce" Ford listened.

■ ■ ■

Whenever my dad got mad at me or my brother, he would never actually hit us. But he did have one of the great belt movements. He'd say, "Do I have to go for the belt?" Then he'd wiggle his waistband around a little—kind of a fatherly Morse code for impending doom. Usually, this was enough to have me say, "Oh, no, Pop! Everything's all right!" Then he'd start pontificating and explain why this one isolated incident of bad behavior would keep me out of college years later. With Dad, it was a matter of disgust. Mom had a different approach that was far more successful. She would come in and hit you, leave for ten minutes, think about it, get even madder, and come back and start hitting you again! I'd ask, "What did I do?" She'd say, "You know what you did!" I'd say, "No, I don't!" And she'd say, "*You know what you did!*" Then I'd just start naming stuff she never even knew about! She would have made a terrific cop. All she needed was a heat lamp.

I was never one to respond well to being yelled at. Fortunately, there wasn't that much yelling in our house. My father would raise his voice, but because he was partially deaf, I figured he just wanted me to *understand* him more clearly. The one time I truly infuriated him was just a few weeks after I'd gotten my driver's license. I had been out driving my mom's '64 Ford Falcon and I turned a corner at a ridiculously high speed. Suddenly, the car rolled over, crushed the roof, then rolled back over onto all four wheels. I was okay, but the head-room was now approximately four inches. I still managed to drive the car home, then went inside and sheepishly told my dad, "Oh, I, uh, had a little accident with the car."

He was very calm. "All right," he said, "let's take a look." He was expecting maybe a broken taillight or a little ding on the fender. We stepped outside and—

"WHAT THE HELL HAPPENED HERE?!"

When you're a kid, you try to diminish your crimes. So I just said, "Uh, the car fell over."

"WHAT DO YOU MEAN IT FELL OVER?! HOW THE HELL DOES A CAR FALL OVER? IT'S SITTING THERE AND THEN IT FELL OVER? IS THAT WHAT YOU'RE TELLING ME?"

"Well, it was slippery and I was on a corner—"

"THE CAR ROLLED OVER ON THE ROOF! THAT IS NOT A DENT!"

And, of course, my mother, who knew nothing about cars, came out and said, "Maybe the car did just fall over . . ."

"IT DIDN'T FALL OVER! THE BOY WAS SPEED-ING!"

"Well," Mom said, "it *could* have fallen over."

That was the angriest I ever made my father. And it didn't help that he developed a slight stoop from driving it in to the body shop.

■　■　■

As I've mentioned, my brother, Pat, is ten years older than me. When I was in high school, he was drafted into the army and sent to Vietnam. We all wanted to keep his spirits up over there, but nobody in the family was much of a letter writer. So my father had the idea to get a tape recorder and ship him voice messages. We went to the electronics store and got one of the new miniature reel-to-reel machines that barely predated cassettes. My father said to the clerk, "My boy is over in Vietnam and we want to send him taped greetings from the family!"

The clerk asked, "How long a tape do you want—fifteen minutes?"

"*Fifteen minutes!* We wouldn't even finish saying hello in fifteen minutes! What's your *longest* tape?"

"Ninety minutes."

"That's more like it! Give me four of those!"

So we brought home the recorder and the tapes and a year's supply of batteries. My father set up everything on the kitchen table and called my mom and me into the room. Very excitedly, he announced, "Okay, now we're all gonna talk to Pat!" He pressed the start button and, in his own inimitable way, began:

"HELLO, PAT! EVERYTHING HERE IS GOOD! I'M FINE! YOUR MOTHER'S FINE! HERE'S YOUR BROTHER! JAMIE, TALK TO PAT!"

I stepped forward: "Hey, Pat! How you doing? Hope you're okay! Be careful over there! Here's Mom!"

Mom bent over the machine and said, "Hello, Pat! Take care of yourself now! Don't do anything silly!"

Then my dad came back: "HEY, WHERE'S BRUCE THE DOG? BRING BRUCE OVER HERE AND MAKE HIM BARK FOR PAT!"

Bruce barked: "Roof roof! Roof roof!"

Then, of course, my father had to point out, "THAT'S THE DOG THERE, PAT! THAT'S BRUCE THE DOG! ALL RIGHT! LET'S PLAY IT BACK!"

We listened to all of about three minutes we put on this ninety-minute tape. The next day, the same thing: "PAT, EVERYTHING IS GOOD! NOT MUCH ELSE IS GOING ON! HERE'S THE DOG!"

"Roof roof! Roof roof!"

After a few weeks, there was no more than nine minutes of tape filled and it was mostly the dog barking. Finally, my father said, "Oh, let's just send the tape! What the hell!" So we shipped the whole contraption off to my brother. Thinking back, I have a feeling he might have preferred a few letters.

■ ■ ■

Having a brother in Vietnam was, of course, a very frightening experience, as many families know. All you can do is hope that no bad news comes. I remember watching television with my mom and dad one Sunday night when we heard a car pull into our driveway. Then we heard the car door open and footsteps coming up the walk. Next our screen door opened and it sounded like something had been thrown into the house. This was all very ominous. My father went to check and came back holding a telegram. Without opening it, he laid the telegram on the dining room table and just stared at it. My mother and I saw this and, slowly, we all sat down around the table, looking at the telegram. Nobody said anything for ten minutes. We just sat there, feeling kind of sick and very scared. Finally, my father reached for the telegram and slit it open. He cleared his throat and began to read aloud:

"Dear Mr. Leno: You are invited to Wentworth Chevrolet to view the exciting new Caprice Classic!"

My father was furious! He never drove a Chevrolet again for the rest of his life.

■　■　■

I always thought my brother was a genius. Only recently, he told me, "You know, I really wasn't all that smart." That made no sense to me. Then again, I was lucky to ever get a C in school. Thus, by contrast, Pat was the family Einstein. He was one of the top ten students at Pennsylvania Military College, then went on to Yale Law School. Whereas I was probably more like my dad, Pat was more like Mom. I have no patience or attention span, but my brother can sit with a butter knife and whittle a piece of wood into almost anything. He made a coffee table for my living room, which looks like it was carved by a Renaissance master. In comparison to him, my idiocy seemed to emerge in much greater relief.

As we've established, I was just a terrible student. Evidence goes back as far as the fifth grade, when my teacher, Mr. Simon, wrote on my report card: "Jay has the ability, but does not apply himself. If Jay spent as much time studying as he does trying to be funny, he would be a great comedian." I guess I had the makings of attention-deficit syndrome. The only time my mind was totally focused and not spinning all over the map, looking for distraction, was when I was being funny. So I started directing this new sharper focus on the execution of absolutely asinine behavior. Or, in other words, stupid school pranks!

One of the classics of the genre was the Faked Suicide, always best employed with substitute teachers. (The unfamiliar are always the most gullible dupes!) This one required an accomplice. Back in junior high, it was Lewis Trumbore. Our school was an enormous old building with huge windows that had to be opened with a pole, so that they would cantilever outward. This would create a gaping space that looked dangerous to begin with. So Lewis's job was to stand by this big window in our third-floor classroom and dangle the heels of my shoes below the ledge. Then he'd holler for the teacher and say in a panicked voice, "Come here quick! Jay Leno's hanging out the window! I can't hold on much longer!"

The teacher would race over, just as Lewis dropped the shoes outside and screamed. Then, the other kids would scream—they had to be in on it to make it work. The teacher would get to the window just in time to look down, clutch her heart, and shriek, "*Oh, my God!*" Of course, I had already been sprawled down on the ground for five minutes, playing dead. And my shoes would be scattered around me. This was always a one-way ticket to the principal's office and a major triumph!

By the time I was in high school, I had perfected a larger repertoire of pranks. A favorite victim was our long-suffering

Gee, which one do you think is me?

janitor, Mr. Swenson, a kindly Swede whose giant rings of keys jangled when he walked. I had a friend with a scrappy little terrier, which he would smuggle into school. To drive Mr. Swenson crazy, on various days, we would hide the dog in different hall lockers. The dog would start yapping. Then we'd go tell Mr. Swenson, who would have to open as many as fifteen lockers to find the barking dog. "Come onnnn-na," he'd mutter. "Which one are you innn-na?" We'd stand back and place bets on how many lockers he would have to open before he found it. And, once he did find it, the dog would leap out and tear down the hall. Then Mr. Swenson would have to run after and try to catch it, which he never did.

Then there was the time I spent six long and dedicated hours gluing together the pages of a dictionary, so that it became one big solid block of a book. (I believe the teacher later hit me on the head with it.) But nothing was more exciting than sneaking into the girls' bathroom and pouring water through the Kotex dispenser. I liked watching the metal machine expand and tear apart from the wall as the napkins absorbed the water. Not only was it very funny, but it would have made a good ad for Kotex.

■　■　■

Let me give you a better idea of the dire nature of my life in academia. I remember one amazing Career Day during my junior year in high school. My mother and I went in to meet with my guidance counselor, who would help us explore my professional possibilities. At the time, I had been working after school at the Andover McDonald's to make extra money. But I had no idea what I'd end up doing with my life. So we sat down with the counselor, who said to my mother, "What does Jay want to do?"

And, as she always believed, she said, "Well, I'm sure he'll go on to college."

The counselor frowned and said, "I know he works at McDonald's after school. Does he like doing that?"

My mom said, "Well, I suppose so. It's just a part-time job, you know."

The counselor cleared his throat. "Well, you know," he said, "*education isn't for everybody, Mrs. Leno.* Sometimes students are better off doing jobs and menial tasks."

My mother just exploded: "*What kind of guidance counselor are you!*"

"Oh, please don't take offense! It's just that the McDonald's people have a program where they send kids to school. I think it's called Hamburger U. Very fine reputation."

Now she was seething. "*He doesn't want to work at McDonald's for the rest of his life!*"

"Well," he said, "it's just an option you might want to consider."

The odd thing was, I was sitting there the whole time. Of course, I wasn't paying much attention. I heard all about this later.

■ ■ ■

Strangely enough, for being a truly bad student, I never missed a day of school. I wasn't much good at actually studying, but I figured I could probably learn through osmosis—just by being present in class every day. Not that it helped all that much. Finally, one April morning in my junior year, I got up and said to my mother, "Ma, I've never missed a day of school. Can I stay home today?"

She began worrying right away: "Well, what if the school calls?"

"They're not gonna call."

"But what if . . ."

"Don't worry! They won't!"

So I stayed home for the first time ever. But, by noon, I got restless and decided to go out for a drive. I had saved enough money from my McDonald's job to buy a new 1965 Buick Grandsport 401 V8—a genuine four-barrel, four-on-the-floor hot rod. (To have this new car in high school was very funny, since all my teachers were driving old DeSotos. No wonder I got lousy grades.) I told my mom, "I'm gonna go out and get some stuff."

She panicked instantly. "Don't go out!" she said. "Somebody might see you!"

"No one's gonna see me."

"Whatever you do—don't go near the high school! They'll see you!"

"Ma, I'm not gonna go to the high school!"

But, like an idiot, I drove uptown past the high school and saw everybody hanging around out front during the lunch hour. So I pulled into the big oval driveway. Kids started to gather

My first new car! As you can see, my fashion sense hasn't changed much.

around my car, shouting, "Hey, Leno! What are you doin'? Ditchin' school? Hey, nice car!" And, being the ridiculous showoff I am, I revved the motor and laid rubber patches. More kids came over, screaming, "Hey, Leno! Burn rubber, man!" So I screeched up and down the driveway and around the parking lot.

Unbeknownst to me, this commotion got the attention of our pudgy little vice-principal, Mr. Adams, who suddenly came running out toward the car. But I never saw him coming. And, just as he got to my rear fender, I popped the clutch and peeled off around the corner with smoke pouring out of the tires! Aside from a few of my friends seeing me, I figured that I'd avoided being spotted. So I drove around for hours with a clear conscience.

Meanwhile, Mr. Adams called my mother, who feared all authority, but this kind especially—actual confrontation. He asked, "Is Jay there?"

"He's . . . uh, sick!" she blurted.

"He's sick? Well, can I speak to him?"

"Well . . . he's in bed resting . . ."

"Is that so? I hate to tell you this, Mrs. Leno, but *he was just here at school burning rubber in the parking lot!*"

And, of course, my mother just burst into tears.

Later on, I came drifting into the house, still pleased that I'd gotten away with my big hooky scheme. I walked in the door, where my mother was waiting for me. From behind her back, she pulled out a big pot and—*CLUNK!*—whacked me on the head. Then she started hollering: "*Why did you go to school?*"

The next thing I knew, we were both sitting in the principal's office. My mother felt like she was about to be deported. The principal lowered the boom: "Jay Leno, consider yourself suspended for three weeks!" He reprimanded me from top to bottom, just an endless stream of pontificating. Then he turned to my mom, who sat there quaking.

"And, worst of all," he said, pointing his finger at her, "YOU—a mother who would LIE!!"

Tears just poured down her face. I think her pot landed on my head a few more times that day.

■ ■ ■

For some unimaginable reason, a handful of my teachers didn't give up on me as a hopeless moron. Mr. Robicheaud, my history teacher, never doubted that I had a brain that was actually functional. He always made me want to rise to any challenge. Same with Ms. Samara, my homeroom teacher. And my English teacher, Mrs. Hawkes, urged me to take her creative writing class. I figured, "What the hell, sounds easy!" But it wasn't—at first, anyway. One day, after class, she took me aside and said, "You know, I always hear you telling funny stories to your friends in class. You should write down some of those stories and we can make that your homework assignment." Hey, it sounded better than poetry!

So I gave it a try and—amazingly—it turned out to be the first time I ever did homework where I wasn't waiting for Ricky Nelson to come on TV. I actually enjoyed it. I'd spend hours writing a story (usually about something stupid that happened at school), reading it to myself, crossing out things that weren't funny. I'd do four or five drafts, then hand it in. Suddenly, it was fun to go to class and stand up to read my funny story— and, best of all, to get some laughs. I was always grateful to Mrs. Hawkes for that.

Another teacher who made a huge impression was Mr. Walsh. For whatever reason, he was always assigned to oversee detention duty in the library. And since I was *always* in detention, we'd sit together almost every day. Mr. Walsh was one of those guys who would laugh at anything. Tell him the simplest joke and he'd break up. Everything was *hilarious* to this man. So I'd have new stories for him all the time. One day he said to me, "Why don't you think about going into show business?"

This was a revelation. The idea never even occurred to me. I didn't know anybody in show business. The closest thing was an eighth-grade teacher named Mr. Duncan, who did magic tricks at student assemblies. And that was *unbelievable*! Someone we knew who could actually *entertain* people! When you grow up in a small town like Andover, show business is the furthest thing from being a career option.

Poor Lyn. When this photo was taken, she was probably thinking, "Oh, nobody will see this."

Jay Leno, with Lyn Deyermond, voted funniest at Andover High in 1968.

But Mr. Walsh's words ignited something in me. I began telling people that I wanted to one day become a comedian. This didn't go over well in the neighborhood. We still lived in a time when, once you had a job, you had a job for life. And comedy wasn't a job in New England. The mother of a friend who lived up the street was quick to discourage me. (Show business is one of those odd professions where people who know nothing about it feel obliged to give you advice.)

As she explained it, "In Hollywood, *you can't be a comedian unless your fatha was a comedian!* Because there's a comedians' union out there! And unless your fatha was a comedian, you can't be a comedian! They won't even let you near a stage!"

Gullible as I was, I thought, "Well, that's it! I'm screwed already! My father wasn't a comedian (although he was pretty funny at insurance conventions). So there's no way I'm going to break into show business." But then I thought, "I don't remember Milton Berle's father being a comedian. Was Lenny Bruce's father a comedian?" I remember walking home thinking, "I don't know *any* comedian whose father was a comedian! I've never heard of that!" It almost works the opposite way. Children of comedians are generally so embarrassed by their fathers that they'd rather sell insurance or do anything else! But when you don't know, you honestly don't know. And I didn't know.

▪ ▪ ▪

Ironic but true: McDonald's was responsible for my career in comedy. All through high school, I had worked at the Andover McDonald's—turning over burgers on the grill, taking food orders, keeping the lot clean. In those days, the french fries had to be hand-cut. So I would sometimes cut up to six hundred pounds of potatoes a day. I became known as the French-Fry Cut-Up—not for my great skill with the dicing machine, but for my unflagging dedication to goofing around with my co-workers.

One day my manager, Tom Curtain, told me about a regional McDonald's talent show. Employees of the stores put on acts and competed for a cash prize. Mr. Curtain said, "Look, you're a funny guy. Why don't you put together a comedy routine for the show?" This seemed like a perfect way to get to tell jokes on a stage (and also test the existence of the alleged comedians' union—would I get rubbed out?). So I got together with a guy named Jay Monroe and started coming up with material. That was the first time I ever tried to write jokes about a specific subject. In this case, the subject was the

McDONALD'S®

APPLICATION FOR EMPLOYMENT

PERSONAL INFORMATION				
DATE *Apri 26, 1966*		SOCIAL SECURITY NUMBER		
NAME *Leno* (LAST) *Jay* (FIRST) *Douglas* (MIDDLE)				AGE *16*
PRESENT ADDRESS *32 Clark Rd* (NO. & STREET) *Andover* (CITY) *Mass* (STATE)				HOW LONG THERE? *7 yrs.*
PREVIOUS ADDRESS (NO. & STREET) (CITY) (STATE)				HOW LONG THERE?
PHONE NO.	OWN HOME	RENT	BOARD	DATE OF BIRTH *1950* HEIGHT *5'*
WEIGHT *164* MARRIED SINGLE *✓* WIDOWED DIVORCED SEPARATED				CITIZEN OF U. S. A.? *✓*
NO. OF CHILDREN	DEPENDENTS OTHER THAN WIFE OR CHILDREN	REFERRED BY		

I went to McDonald's, since I flunked the test to get into Woolworth's.

world of McDonald's—a staple for every comedian of my generation.

At that point in the late sixties, McDonald's was phasing out its red-and-white-tiled stores and replacing them with the brown town houses under the golden arches. The Andover store happened to be one of the last of the tiled storefronts left. So this was one of the jokes we told at the talent show: "Our manager, Mr. Curtain, is a very farsighted individual. He just bought a hundred thousand cases of red-and-white tiles because he wants to expand!" For this, we got screams of laughter. Believe it or not. We also won the competition and the $150 cash prize. That was my first glimmer that money could be made by telling jokes. All thanks to McDonald's. Of course, I've tried to repay them ever since by doing McDonald's jokes throughout my career, and nowadays on *The Tonight Show*. I'm not sure they see this as a debt of gratitude.

4

JAMIE ONNA DA STAGE!

Ollege was a mystery to me. It was something I was supposed to do, something my parents wanted me to do—and something I had no idea how to do. But there was a war on, which was another good reason to seek some kind of higher learning. Unfortunately, my high school grade point average couldn't have been lower—like a festival of F's—placing my learning potential on the scale somewhere between Intelligence-Impaired and Hapless Moron. For some ridiculous reason, I entered the Bentley School of Accounting and Finance, which seemed like a solid pursuit, even though I had no idea what anybody there was ever talking about. (Having a fairly problematic case of dyslexia, I usually see numbers backwards, which could have made for some very entertaining profit-loss tabulations.) But they accepted my tuition money and, suddenly, I was trapped in a very wrong place.

It didn't last long. I remember sitting in some math class

that I was flunking miserably. The professor was rambling on about theorems and whatnot, and he asked me a question that completely eluded me. I jolted awake from my perpetual nap and, thinking fast, I cleverly turned the tables. I said, "First, *I* have a question for *you:* I've always wondered about math—just the whole concept of it. Who is the person responsible?" The professor simply glared at me and said, "Mr. Leno, your time-wasting techniques are growing very tiresome. Why don't you just get out right now!" (I have a feeling that he didn't know the answer to my question, anyway.)

■　■　■

I next set my sights on Emerson College, an esteemed Boston school that specialized in theatrical and communication arts. I figured this was as good a place as any to prepare to become a comedian. Of course, they wanted nothing to do with me. Emerson's dean of admissions looked at my dismal high school record and burst out laughing. This wasn't necessarily a bad thing, since I told him I aspired to make people laugh for a living. But he wasn't exactly amused. "Your grades don't indicate that you have much incentive," he told me. "You're not really what we're looking for." But I didn't give up. I just stalked the guy.

For the next three days, I would sit outside his office from eight in the morning until he went home at five. Finally, at the end of the third day, he said, "You really want to go here?" I told him yes. Duh. So he heaved a sigh and said, "All right, take some summer school courses." I said, "Great! How much is summer school?" He said twelve hundred bucks, thinking maybe that this would intimidate me. Fortunately, I used to carry a lot of cash in those days. I pulled out twelve hundred-dollar bills in a big wad and handed them over. The dean gave me a long look and said, "All right, you're in." And that was the extent of my college entrance program. The dean probably thought I was a mobster. Not that it helped my grades. Maybe I should have tipped him.

■ ■ ■

One of my first courses at Emerson was television production, where we were supposed to learn the basics of broadcasting. On the first day of class, I knew something was peculiar. The teacher began things by saying to us, "Are you all familiar with Dan Rather, the newsman? Well, he got his big break covering a hurricane and he had to go on camera *immediately* and start reporting the story. In the broadcast field, *any one of you* could be called upon to broadcast—AT ANY TIME! Even if you're not regular on-air talent, there might be an emergency. So, of course, you always want to look your best! It's very important."

With that, he started handing out these Max Factor makeup kits. "The first thing we want to do," he said, "is to practice putting on makeup!"

We opened up these kits and he moved around the room, giving tips: "Okay, good, Bob! Try a little more foundation!" He was daubing us with his eyebrow pencil and helping girls apply lipstick! Suddenly, the whole class looked like the road company of *La Cage aux Folles*. I have a hard time believing that Dan Rather ever did this before that hurricane. And, if he had, wouldn't the hurricane have pretty much obliterated his makeup? Still, I was so glad we were covering the hard-hitting fundamentals of broadcasting.

■ ■ ■

I've often said that the reason I chose Emerson was that most
of the exams were oral. I could give a talk instead of take a test,
which I figured would tremendously improve my chances of
not flunking. This didn't exactly hold true. My grades stunk,
anyway. Then, one semester, something amazing happened. As
part of the liberal tenor of the times, Emerson decided to try a
progressive idea. For this particular semester, students were
instructed to grade themselves. That is, we could give ourselves the grades we thought we deserved.

Naturally, I was thrilled. "This," I thought, "is my opportunity! My ship has come in!"

I had never gotten an A in my life. So, for every course, I
gave myself an A. Not an A-plus. Not an A-minus. Just A's
across the board. I had never seen anything so beautiful. The
next thing I knew, I was on the dean's list!

I proudly brought the semester report card home to my
father, who beamed. "*I knew you could do it! I knew my boy could
do it!*"

I said, "Thank you, Pop! It took a lot of hard work!"

He started telling everybody he ever knew: "Look at this!
Straight A's! My son! And they said he'd never go to college!
Straight A's!" People from his office were calling me, saying,
"Congratulations! Your father is so proud of you!"

And I'd say, "Well, it took a lot of hard work, I'll tell you."

Then, of course, the next semester came around and I was
back to my usual D's and F's. Sadly, I brought that report card
home, too.

My father looked at it and said, "WHAT THE HELL DID
YOU DO?"

"I don't know, Dad. I don't know what happened."

"BUT YOU GOT STRAIGHT A'S LAST TIME!"

"I don't know, Pop. It was harder this year."

Then, because he never really grasped how these things worked, he would insist on signing the report card. I told him, "Dad, this is college! You don't have to sign report cards!"

"How will the teacher know I saw it?" he'd say.

"Dad, they don't care if you see it!"

But he always signed it and mailed it back to the school. Humiliation can be a repeat offense.

■ ■ ■

I had heard about a strange new business in Boston that sold term papers. This made perfect sense to me: Why write a term paper when you could buy one? They could create any kind of report imaginable. So I went down to their office and asked how much a term paper cost. The guy there said, "Well, what grade do you want?"

"Well, I'm a conscientious guy. I want to be a good student," I said. "I'd like an A."

The guy said an A would cost a hundred dollars. And, for another ten bucks, they would type up a beautiful title page with my name, the teacher's name, the course number—just to legitimize the whole thing. So I happily paid the price, figuring it was money well spent, got my paper, and turned it in.

A week later, I was sitting in class, staring out the window, as usual. With a disgusted expression, the teacher began to pass back the graded term papers. "This class has not applied itself," she groaned. "These term papers are uniformly terrible! But, quite frankly, there is one exception. I am pleasantly surprised by the effort of one student, Jay Leno. Your paper was excellent—you get an A."

Naturally, I swelled with pride and said, "Oh, thank you. Thank you very much." This was just unbelievable! A little too unbelievable, it turned out.

Later on in class, I was staring out the window, half-asleep, but still feeling like a genius. Suddenly, I heard the teacher say, "Jay, let me ask you about hotel/motel management." This seemed like an odd topic to cover in a writing class.

I said, "Me?"

"What do you know about hotel/motel management?"

"Uh, hotel/motel management? I don't know anything about it."

"You have no interest in it?" she asked.

"No, it's not really anything I'd be interested in."

With that, she ran over and grabbed back my term paper and ripped it to bits.

"Well," she screamed, "you wrote a term paper about it and got an A!"

I said, "*Oh, I did? Yes, that's right!*"

She just said, "F! Get out!"

I was such an idiot that I didn't even read the paper that I'd bought! Let me tell you, that was an invaluable lesson learned the hard way. From then on I knew: Better to get an F—and save a hundred and ten dollars.

■ ■ ■

During my first year at college, I lived in a small dormitory, where I met a very funny guy named Gene Braunstein. He now lives in Los Angeles, where he writes television comedy, and

Hey, we're in showbiz! Gene & Jay's Unique and Original Comedy now appearing at the Nameless Coffeehouse in Harvard Square.

we still talk all the time. Back then, we quickly discovered our mutual love for comedians and became instant friends. In the dorm, we started writing bits together, which we would try out in local coffeehouses. I think I was drawn to Gene as a comedy partner because he sounded like Dick Cavett. Very wry and smart. A perfect straight man. As opposed to me: Apparently, I was sort of the Loud Guy.

Anyway, these coffeehouses where we worked were very much Of That Era—post-beatnik havens for protesters of every kind. There was the Orson Welles Theater Café, the Sword in the Stone, the Café Wah, and the Nameless Coffeehouse in Harvard Square—the place where Gene and I debuted our comedy act. We billed ourselves as Gene & Jay's

Unique and Original Comedy. That night, as almost always, we followed some angry guy reading poems that invariably seemed to end with the same line: "Stop your war machines!" The audience would then hoot and applaud wildly. And the angry poet would gush, "Thank you, thank you, ladies and gentlemen!" It was all very incongruous.

But it got even more incongruous when we took the stage. For the first time ever, Gene and I performed a bit we called the Loan Arranger. The stupid premise was simple enough: Tonto goes to the bank to take out a loan. I played Tonto and it went like this:

"Me want loan."

"Yes, sir, I'm the loan arranger."

"You Lone Ranger?"

"No, loan *arranger*."

"Lone Ranger?"

"No, loan arranger. *I arrange the loans*."

It was that bad. But it was also our first time. And not three minutes into it a woman in the audience screamed at us: "Hey, you're being cruel and insensitive to Native Americans! Many Native Americans suffer under the hands of oppression."

She stopped us cold. I said, "It's just a bit about the Lone Ranger and Tonto!"

"Yes, but by making fun of Tonto, you're making fun of all Native Americans."

I said, "It's just a guy going for a loan! The joke is not the Indian. It's mistaken identity, not—"

"That doesn't matter!"

Suddenly, my first real gig in comedy had turned into a civil rights rally! Later, however, we revised the bit and had

Tonto say things like "Nixon, *what a jerk!* Stop your war machines! Thank you! Good night!" It wasn't any funnier, but the applause was tremendous.

▪ ▪ ▪

Of the two of us, "Geno" was more of the hippie guy. He loved the psychedelic music and enjoyed smoking a little dope. I was sort of the clean-cut guy. I somehow missed the urge to ever get stoned—to this day, my total alcoholic consumption is half a glass of beer. I couldn't finish it. I can't even eat rum cake. I just never liked to lose my edge. Although old photographs might suggest otherwise: Like everybody else, I had long hair and wore little wire-rimmed granny glasses, big vests, and snap-brim hats. To affect a sophisticated air in college, I even took up pipe smoking, which probably made me look even dorkier.

But, as with most teams, our differences worked well together. In my second year at Emerson, we moved off campus

Gee, I wonder why I wasn't getting any work?

to an apartment on Commonwealth Avenue. About that same time, I remember we went to see the movie *Joe*, in which Peter Boyle hated hippies so much that he stalked them with a gun. This really shook up Geno, whose friends mostly tended to be hippies. Shortly afterward, in fact, he told me that a few of his friends from back home were coming to visit and would be staying in the apartment. He warned me that they were big dope smokers, which was fine. Most everybody else was.

Because they hadn't yet met me, I thought it would be hilarious to terrorize them, *Joe*-style. The first night they were at the apartment, I knew they'd all be hanging out, drinking wine and smoking dope. So I went out and bought a starter's pistol, the kind that sounds a very loud cap-fire to begin track races. I decided to make a dramatic entrance. I waited for my moment, then kicked in the door and shouted, "*HIPPIES!*"

I assumed the squat position and started firing the pistol at them. They all leaped five feet in the air! One guy, who was completely stoned, just shrieked—"YAAAAAAAGGGGH-HHHHH!" His hair visibly turned white before me. Then he climbed behind the couch, crying and sniveling. I walked over to him and extended my hand.

I said, "Hi, I'm Jay, Gene's roommate. Glad to meet you."

He whimpered, "Just don't kill me, man!"

They all managed to recover somewhat. In fact, they later tried to use the starter pistol as a bong.

But there is a postscript: Eighteen years after that incident, I bumped into the same guy who climbed behind the couch. By now, he was a successful businessman, married with kids.

I said, "Hi, Bob, remember me?"

And he said, "YAAAAAAAGGGHHHHHHHH!"

■ ■ ■

Once, there were no young comedians. It seems almost unfath-omable now. But standup comedy had never really been a young man's game. The comedians you saw on the *Ed Sullivan Show* were middle-aged, primarily Jewish, native New Yorkers—all grown men in nice suits, like Alan King and Rodney Dangerfield. Their material tended to speak more to your father than to you. Although there would always be the obligatory crumb thrown: "*Hey, how 'bout these crazy kids today!*"

In Boston, there were no comedians at all. At least, I never met one. But, at that point, there was no such thing as a com-edy club, either. Looking back, that was probably advanta-geous for me. Today, new comics living in Los Angeles have to compete with famous names like Jerry Seinfeld and Larry Miller and Robin Williams for stage time at clubs. No matter how well the new comedians do, they're still going to be over-shadowed. Makes it tougher to get noticed.

The forerunners of my generation began turning up at the end of the sixties: David Steinberg, George Carlin, Robert Klein. If I had one major influence, it was Klein. His back-ground seemed similar to mine. Just a guy raised by a normal middle-class family. His points of reference were the same as mine: current television, pop culture, mass media, and the ridiculous details of a young person's everyday life. And this was a revelation to me.

Carlin and Steinberg were the same way. In fact, I memo-rized Carlin's marvelous Class Clown routine and would run it through my head before making extemporaneous class speeches at Emerson, just to jump-start myself. I'd have his comedic rhythm playing in the back of my head—a proven, wonderful rhythm that I tried to emulate. This always worked much better than starting cold. I did, however, stop short of wearing the Carlin ponytail.

Whenever big comedians came through Boston, Gene Braunstein and I always tried to go catch their acts. Usually, they'd work the Playboy Club and a great club called Paul's Mall, where we saw Flip Wilson, Cheech & Chong, Robert Klein, and David Steinberg. Steinberg even let us interview him for our college radio station and took the time to encourage us. In fact, despite the cutthroat reputation of comedians, I was never discouraged by anybody in the business. Nobody ever said, "Forget it! Get the hell out now!"

Except once.

I took a part-time job washing dishes at the Boston Playboy Club. I figured this would be my surefire entrée into the exciting world of professional show business. The logic was: Maybe if I started out as a dishwasher, I could somehow graduate to become the headline comedian in the Playmate Room! Obviously, I was an idiot. And this was a terrible job. I worked under Rodney the cook, an enormous black man who must have weighed three hundred pounds. A very jovial, nice guy, but all business. Rodney set me up in front of these vast washbasins piled high with hundreds of filthy plates. I would shoot a sprayer of scalding water at the mountain of plates—plates that never stopped piling up. Every five minutes, another hundred plates would come in. This was a task with no real sense of accomplishment. The minutes felt like hours. After a few weeks, I had to quit.

But I did derive some pleasure from the job. Occasionally I would stick my head into the showroom to watch comedians.

Then, inevitably, Rodney would catch me and holler, "What are you doing? Get back to work!" During an early break one night, I managed to sneak into the showroom when Rodney wasn't around. It was completely empty. Nobody was in sight. I decided this was my moment. I wanted to go stand on the stage and know what that felt like. I crept up there and stood in front of the mike, which was shut off. So I started goofing around, doing pretend patter: *"Hey, how's everybody doin' tonight? You look like a great crowd!"*

And that's when I saw the comedian Stuey Stone—who's still working today—step out of the wings. He was that night's headliner and he looked angry.

He shouted, "Hey, what are you doing?"

I said, "I want to be a comedian. I just thought I'd—"

"Well, you get off that stage! That stage is for *professional comedians only!*"

Then he launched into a long lecture that seemed to go on for an eternity. He tore into me. To this day, I'm still not sure whether he was kidding. But I took it seriously. When you're starting out in show business, even the smallest, most insignificant slights have monumental consequences. And Stuey Stone's tirade had lasting impact. To this day, whenever I meet someone interested in comedy, I always try to encourage him or her. God forbid that that kid would later write a book like this! I don't ever want to read, "And Leno told me to get out of the business—that idiot!"

■ ■ ■

Braunstein and I saw an advertisement in the newspaper that said: "DO YOU THINK YOU'RE FUNNY? CALL THIS

NUMBER." It smelled like a dare, so we called. It turned out to be an audition for a comedy troupe with the very unfunny name Fresh Fruit Cocktail. On a lark, we went down to audition and, amazingly, I was chosen and Geno wasn't. (They needed a Loud Guy, I reasoned.) Ultimately, being part of a group wasn't very satisfying. Some people wanted to work and others didn't. We would do bits and little improvisations. But, for the most part, everyone had his own ideas and there were just too many different kinds of comedy clashing. Still, it was fun while it lasted—which for me was about six months.

The best part of the whole experience was being booked to play the Playboy Club. Before our first show, Rodney the cook spotted me, and—even though months had passed since I quit—out of reflex, he shouted, "Hey, get back in the kitchen!"

I said, "No, Rodney, I'm *working* up here!"

"Yeah, shut up! We got dishes to wash!"

He didn't believe me. Of course, there *were* moments during that night's performance when I wished that I'd listened to him.

■ ■ ■

After leaving Fresh Fruit Cocktail, I decided that it was time to create my own act. It was time to be a comedian. Not that I had all that much time between classwork at Emerson. But I knew there were places in New York where comedians could try out material between music acts and more angry poets. One night I would make the four-hour drive and just go do it. So I sat down to write my first joke, which was based on my own experience and which I ended up using for years. For better or worse, with my apologies, here it is:

The improv group Fresh Fruit Cocktail. Though we were only together for six months, we're still friends. In fact, Bob Perlo, second from the left, still works with me on The Tonight Show.

Boston is a big college town. A lot of people think it's very hip, very liberal, very permissive. And it is! In a lot of ways—except one! I go to school there and in my dormitory, you can have girls in your room. You can have liquor in your room. You can have drugs in your room twenty-four hours a day if you want to! There's only one thing you're not allowed to have: a hot plate!

One night, not too long ago, I went back to my room and

there was my roommate, his girlfriend, and her roommate lying on
the bed. He's got five joints in his mouth. There's an empty bottle
of apple wine on the floor. He's passed out cold. I figure, "Well,
it's quiet, at least. I'll do a little studying." After about ten
minutes, I get hungry, sneak out my hot plate, decide to cook
some soup.

Next thing I know, I hear a knock at the door!
"What's going on in there?"
"Oh, nothing, nothing, sir!"
More knocking: "You got soup in there?"
"No, sir! All we've got in here are women, liquor, and drugs!"
"Don't lie to me, son. I know you have soup in there!"

A guy has to start someplace.

■ ■ ■

So I started at a place in Greenwich Village called the Bitter
End. Everyone from Lenny Bruce to George Carlin had played
the Bitter End, which made the adventure an even bigger deal
to me. I drove down from Boston for an audition night, ready
to try out my stuff. The only problem was that I had an
extremely sore throat and it hurt to even open my mouth.
Somebody backstage handed me a bottle of Chloraseptic
throat spray and said, "This will help." The pain was so
intense, I figured I'd better take an extra dose, so I spritzed my
mouth about ten times.

Unfortunately, nobody told me that Chloraseptic has a
kind of numbing effect and makes your tongue feel thick, as
though it's encased in cotton. Now I couldn't speak intelligi-
bly!

So I got up to do my audition and this is roughly what came out of my mouth:

"Hhhmmmmhhhhh rrrrhhn ssprrpfffxx wnnnhhhhffffnnn bbbrrmmmmffff . . ."

Afterward, Ted Lorenz, who ran the club, came over and said, "Well, it sounded like you had some funny stuff there. But people can't understand what you're saying. Do you have a lisp or something?"

I said, "Nnnohh, Ahhh hahhvvve sohrrrre thhhhhrroat. Tookkkk sohmmme Chlrrrrsssseptccck!"

He said, "Well, just come back next week when you feel better."

The next week, I felt better and the material seemed to work okay. This time, Ted said, "You did good. You can come back in a week and work for free." (That, of course, is standard policy when you start out.) Before I left the club, I was approached by a guy who turned out to be a small-time press agent.

He said, "Hey, great! You're back next week! You need a P.R. guy to handle this for you!"

I said, "What do you mean?"

He said, "You need to get the word out that you're going to be here."

Sounded okay to me, so I said, "Well, what do I have to do?"

He said, "I'll take care of it."

The following week, I came into the club, which, of course, was empty as ever. Not that I really expected otherwise. People didn't exactly rush out to watch amateurs. But the press agent was waiting for me. He handed me a bill and said, "You owe me a hundred and fifty bucks."

I looked at the bill, which said: "Placed ad in the

Pennysaver—$50. Put up fliers—$25. Representation fee—$75." I said to him, "You never said I'd have to pay you this much!"

He started screaming, "Hey, you hired me! You told me to do this!" And he went to complain to Ted Lorenz. So, like an idiot, I just paid him. He took the money and stormed away, saying, "I don't want to be your P.R. guy anymore!"

Despite this crushing blow, I went on that night and, again, managed to do well enough to be asked back the following week. This was starting to get exciting, so I called my folks and told them the good news. My dad, of course, was just thrilled that I was doing well in any endeavor—even standup comedy. So, unbeknownst to me, he called up all the Italian relatives in New York and told them, "Jay's gonna be in a club in the Village next week! Go see him!"

That night, I walked in and, as usual, there was only a handful of people in the audience. I went backstage to wait my turn and, suddenly, I heard a big commotion out front. Then I recognized a loud voice saying, "HEY! IS JAY LENO GONNA BE HERE TONIGHT?!" It had to be my Uncle Lou. Which it was. Peeking out from behind the curtain, I saw him bustling into the room with my ninety-year-old grandmother, who spoke no English, as well as my Uncle Mike and his two daughters, who were nine and twelve. They all sat down at a table to watch the other acts, some of which were so filthy you literally had to be a gynecologist to understand them.

Already, I was mortified. Then Uncle Lou started making a ruckus. Lou has always been the great character of the family. A lifelong bachelor, he has a kind of George Raft look, always decked out in a big coat and fedora. At one point, he even owned racehorses. Now I heard him holler for a waitress, saying, "HEY, I NEED A SCOTCH AND SODA HERE!" She told him that all they served was herbal tea. "WHAT THE HELL IS HERBAL TEA? JUST GIVE ME ONE OF THOSE!"

Meanwhile, some hippie folk guitar player had taken the stage to sing war protest songs. The waitress brought Lou his herbal tea and he started bellowing, "WHAT THE HELL KIND OF DRINK IS THIS?" This was a nightmare. Ted Lorenz sidled up to me and said, "Who *are* those people?" Completely embarrassed, I said, "It's my family. They came down to see my debut." Then the folksinger came offstage, complaining to Ted, "I thought this was supposed to be a hip place!" I gulped and said, "That's my family. Will you take it easy? They can't help it."

My turn to go onstage: I walked out and heard, "*HEY, JAY! HEY, JAY BABY!*" My family applauded wildly—in contrast to the handful of other customers, who couldn't have been less interested. And, of course, every other act in the place just *hated* me now. Meanwhile, my grandma, who had no idea what was going on, just kept saying, "*Jamie onna da stage! Jamie onna da stage!*"

Somehow I guess I did my act. I don't remember much about it, except seeing an angry look on my Uncle Mike's face throughout the whole set. Mike was the most religious member of the family, and I guess my material was a little raw in places. One particularly bad joke was about a new male hygiene spray called Umpire: I said it was made specifically For Men With Foul Balls! Uncle Mike just glowered at me.

Then he made my cousins cover their ears for the rest of the show.

5

I NEED A CUT MAN

ack in Boston, I discovered that great starting ground for so many comics: strip clubs! Since the early days of burlesque, these places always had a guy come out and tell jokes between every dancer's turn onstage. I guess it was supposed to break the horrible monotony of ogling bare flesh. For a nineteen-year-old college student, of course, this was a simply *wonderful* job: I had naked women at my work! What could be better? Show business was just getting more thrilling by the day! My friends were toiling at fry-cook jobs where they were getting splattered with peanut oil. I was making twenty bucks a night and fraternizing with wanton women. I felt like I was in the Rat Pack.

I worked at the Teddy Bear Lounge, next door to the Playboy Club. The first woman I remember opening for was called Miss Cow—in reference to her very obvious attributes. These strippers liked to consider themselves exotic dancers. But they were enormous women—big breasts, big hips—sort of like Russian peasants. Onstage, they appeared to be very good-looking. Offstage, I'd see them without their wigs and scarlet rouge—and could hardly recognize them. None of them were hookers, either. They were real working-class women, who made upward of a thousand dollars a week dancing. And they were truly wonderful characters.

My favorites were two nice women called Lily Pagan and Anita Mann (as in "I-need-a-man"). They took an immediate liking to me—being this sort of innocent punk—and acted like my protective big sisters. You would see them drive around in a pink Nash on the doors of which they'd emblazoned pictures of themselves lying on their backs. Somehow this made the car look like a giant pink air freshener. Often they would do shows outside military bases like Fort Devin. I'd watch them build their stages, hauling wood, pounding nails, then setting up big Plexiglas tubs that looked like champagne glasses. Part of their act was to take naked bubble baths inside the champagne glass, draping their legs over the rim, and contort themselves in every which way. Then I would do my act in front of these glasses, as they squirmed around behind me.

One time, at the Teddy Bear Lounge, I was performing my miserable material, which was of course the last thing anybody in the audience cared about. I'd go, "*Hey, Nixon, what a jerk!*" Servicemen on leave would scream back, "Hey! He's the president! Shut up!" Then I'd do a joke about a commercial for an audience applause school: "'We'll teach you how to laugh and applaud like those big-time audiences on TV!'" This was just wishful thinking. One guy started shouting, "You suck! Get off! You stink!" And he wouldn't stop. Then I heard some splashing behind me.

I turned and saw one of the women climb out of her champagne glass, dripping with bubbles. She walked over to the guy who was yelling at me, grabbed him by the collar, and just pounded him in the face. Blood spurted out of his nose. Then she came back to the stage and climbed back into her glass, while the other women cheered, "Yeah! Go get 'em, Lily!"

That was the first time in my life that a nude woman had to defend my honor. Sadly, these opportunities don't occur often enough.

Looking back, I'm still amazed at my naïveté around these women. Besides the older strippers at the Teddy Bear Lounge, younger dancers would come through and work for a while. I had noticed one very pretty girl in her early twenties, of whom another stripper told me, "I think Silver likes you." I was flabbergasted. And excited. So, one night, I knocked on her dressing-room door. She called out, "Come on in." And she was standing there *completely naked!*

She smiled and told me to sit down, which I did. Then she stood over me and hoisted one of her legs up on the arm of the sofa, where I was sitting. Which provided me with an astonishing view—had I bothered to notice. Oblivious to what was looming before my eyes—and, moreover, to what this suggested—I tried to make pleasant conversation. I said, "So, how are ya doin'?"

"Good."

I made a little more small talk, then very timidly said, "Hey, um, can I get your phone number . . . maybe call ya sometime?"

She said, a little impatiently, "Uh, yeah, okay." And she wrote down her phone number.

I took the number and rushed out of the dressing room like an idiot! All that mattered was that I had gotten a girl's phone number! It didn't even occur to me that she was hitting on *me*. I just didn't want to be too forward with a naked stripper who dangled her private parts in my face! For some reason, she must have sensed my general ineptitude. She never did go out with me.

■ ■ ■

These strip clubs would often host amateur nights, which always gave the men a big thrill. The idea of a woman stepping out of the audience and improvising her own striptease seemed terribly provocative. In reality, most of the women who did this were professional strippers only pretending to be first-time exhibitionists. But I'll never forget one particular night when a woman who did this *truly* was an amateur.

She came up from the audience and looked very nervous. She was wearing tight jeans, cowboy boots, and a tiny top. She started her dance, got her top off, and swung it around her head in the clumsiest fashion. Then she went for her jeans, which she got down to her ankles, then her panties, but suddenly she was struggling to get them over her cowboy boots. She tried to step out of the jeans, but she fell backwards and hit her head on the floor and was knocked unconscious! She just lay there, half-naked, while the music kept playing.

Then the emcee, trying to cover it up, hollered, "How about that, ladies and gentlemen! Isn't she fabulous!" He walked over, took her by the knotted-up ankles, and nonchalantly dragged her offstage, with her head bouncing on the floor all the way. This was the most humiliating thing I'd ever seen. The guys in the audience just kept on hooting. And I thought that being a comic was dangerous.

■   ■   ■

One night at the strip club, a man approached me after a show. He said, "Hey, you ever do private gigs? I've got a little place in Dorchester." Dorchester is a working-class Boston suburb full of double- and triple-decker houses. This guy said he ran a small private club in a home there. He asked me to come by late the next afternoon and start performing. It sounded a little odd, but, naturally, I was available for any work, so I took the job.

The next day, I drove to the house, which looked like any other house on the street, except there were a bunch of cars parked outside. The man led me into the living room, which was full of crappy old furniture and dilapidated couches. There were five guys sitting around, looking very uncomfortable. I was immediately intimidated. I was nineteen—facing a small group of real he-men! They looked like the kind of high-testosterone guys who, when they shaved, they probably had to shave again right away. Some of them had lunch pails. They were smoking and not making any kind of eye contact with one another. They just kind of looked down at the floor.

I turned to the man who hired me and said, "What is this? There are only five guys here—"

He said, "That's all right. It's a little men's club. Just do your show for them."

Then, very slowly, it began to occur to me that this guy was running a whorehouse. The girls were upstairs and the men would wait downstairs for their turns. It was like some New

Orleans bordello, transplanted to a Boston suburb. There was even a movie projector and screen, which must have been for showing stag films. But now this guy must have decided that it would be a nice touch to have a comedian entertain customers while they waited.

So, with no introduction, I cleared my throat and started my act:

"Uh, how you guys doin' tonight? Hey, ever been to McDonald's? Ever notice when you go into—"

At this point, one particularly burly guy looked up at me and said, "Hey, what are you doing?"

I said, "I'm a comedian and the boss wanted me to entertain you guys."

"What? You're gonna entertain us? Get the hell outta here!"

"But—"

"GET OUTTA HERE! GET OUTTA HERE!"

I just ran out the door and never turned back. I didn't even want to get paid, which is really saying something. But I figured that if money had changed hands, I'd still be trying to explain my prostitution record.

▪ ▪ ▪

In search of other venues, I learned that the state of Massachusetts would pay ten bucks for performances at retirement homes and certain prison wards. It wasn't exactly Vegas, but at least the audiences were breathing. (Then again, the stench of urine and disinfectant in these places made breathing an option worth reconsidering.) A comedian friend of mine named Bob Shaw, who later went on to write *Seinfeld* shows, would go with me on some of these gigs.

I remember one old people's home, where we had gone to play for a woman's ninetieth birthday. We set up in the rec room, and the little old woman was wheeled in to watch us. The nurse told her, "Bessie, we have these nice comedians here for you today!" She gave a big smile and Shaw started his material, which was always a little blue, in the vein of Lenny Bruce. And, on that day, his jokes kept getting dirtier and dirtier. The old woman was visibly quaking—and repulsed.

"Well, Bessie," Shaw was saying, "have you heard about the new laxative on the market now? Supposed to be great! It's called *Nepo Eloh*, which if spelled backwards is *Open Hole!*"

At that moment, Bessie *leaped* from her wheelchair, grabbed Shaw by the throat, and started throttling him. "Enough! Enough!" she screamed. She looked like a little rag doll, her legs and arms flying in all directions. It took two orderlies to get her off Shaw and back into the wheelchair. But I guess there was some good news: Before this, nobody thought she would walk again.

Literally, the toughest crowds were always the ones in prison. We played Walpole State Prison—an experience that's forever etched in my memory. There's nothing quite like trying to entertain somewhat deranged, hardened criminals who require armed guards to restrain them from killing you. This gave new and unfortunate meaning to the term *dying onstage*. Strangely, the only material that seemed effective with these guys were stories about my mom. (Even cons have mothers—as their many tattoos evidenced.) But I'd pretend they were like any other audience and start out saying, "Hey, hi there, everybody! How you doin'?" And invariably someone would let go of a bloodcurdling scream—"Aaaaggggggghhhhhh!"

Then a guard would drag him off to the hole or some such confinement.

During one prison show, I couldn't help but notice a convict in the front row. He was huge and intimidating and, worse, he was holding another guy on a choke chain. The guy on the chain was this young, dazed-looking kid in his underpants. He sat at the feet of the big convict, who would jerk the leash every few minutes. Obviously, this kid probably got caught with a joint in his sock and wound up being an indentured slave for the next six years. Not the ideal audience.

The only thing worse was playing psychiatric hospitals. These were audiences of schizophrenics and people in straitjackets for whom you just felt terribly sorry. But I will never know a greater challenge than trying to get laughs from someone when he's chained to the wall, naked, sitting in his own urine.

■ ■ ■

When you start out in show business, you never know when you're dealing with legitimate people. More often than not, you invariably get taken for a ride of some humiliating sort. I remember going around Boston's Combat Zone, from strip club to strip club, looking for standup work. One day, I walked into a place and asked to talk to the owner. I was sent to his office, where I found him behind his desk. On top of the desk was a girl, and he actually had his hand wedged up her skirt! He removed it only to shake my hand, then put it back for the rest of our conversation.

"What do you want?"

I said, "I'm a comedian."

"Comedian?" He looked at the girl, chomped his cigar, and moved his hand around in the skirt. "What kind of comedian are you?"

I told him I'd worked in an improvisation group and done some standup in New York and around town.

He said, "Are you in the union?"

I said no.

"Well, how long have you been a comedian?"

I said, "Six months."

"Six months? You gotta be in the union within ninety days! You're in violation already! I could turn you in!"

I couldn't tell whether he was kidding. I said, "Well, I didn't know . . ."

"You gotta be in the union! I can't hire you! I can't even be talking to you! You gotta join. Here, go see this guy and he'll put you in the union."

With his free hand, he gave me a card with the name of someone across town. So I took the card and went to see the other guy, who was ensconced in a typical old show biz office with yellowed pictures of Milton Berle and various celebrities on the wall. I told him that the club owner had sent me over to join the union. The same conversation followed: How long had I been working? I was supposed to join the union after ninety days. I could be fined. Long speech. Finally, I asked what it cost to join the union.

"Five hundred dollars."

I said, "I don't have five hundred dollars."

Then came that classic line: "Well, how much do you have?"

I reached into my pocket and pulled out everything, which was about seventy-three bucks.

The guy said, "Okay, give me that." He took the money and, rather than put it somewhere on his desk, he just stuffed it into his pants. Then he got one of his business cards and wrote out the words "Union Man," then signed his name. He handed it to me.

"Just show this," he said.

I said, "But what about the rest of the money?"

He said, "Well, you'll pay as you get more work. But, from this day forth, you're in the union." And he kind of hustled me out the door.

So I went back to the strip joint and found the owner and his missing hand. He asked, "So how'd you make out?"

I said, "I joined."

He broke out in a big grin. "You joined? How much did it cost you?"

I said, "I only had seventy-three bucks, but I got this card."

The guy just started chuckling to himself and said, "Oh, boy, that Bill is something, isn't he!" Then he said, "Well, I don't have any work for you right now, but congratulations, Union Man! Good luck to you."

I slunk out of there, knowing that I'd been ripped off. I felt so violated. And he didn't even have to put his hand up my skirt to do it.

▪ ▪ ▪

To avoid further humiliation, I thought that I'd better get a manager. The Boston phone book listed only one theatrical manager. I went to see him and knew I was in trouble when I saw his walls covered with pictures of wrestlers. He asked me what my line of work was. I said I was a comedian.

It was as though I'd hit him with a plank. "Standup comedy? There's no money in that! That's stupid! That's nowhere! *That's nowhere!*"

Then he looked at me, up and down and sideways, and brightened. He said, "Hey, you're a big kid. You ever wrestle?"

I said, "Well, I wrestled in high school gym class a little bit, and also at the Y a couple of times."

He rubbed his hands together excitedly and said, "Good, good. Listen, I'll tell you what: You can be Comedy Man! Here's what you do. You get in the ring and when you get a guy in a hold—you whisper a joke in his ear! The guy laughs and then you pin him!"

I said, "Oh, I don't know. It's a little different from what I had in mind . . ."

He didn't want to hear it: "You ain't gonna get anywhere with that standup crap! Just forget that now. Be Comedy Man and, I'm telling you, you'd make a fortune! And the best part is, no one will ever know the jokes you tell! You don't have to tell them to the audience—just the other wrestler! Just whisper into his ear and he falls down! Boom!"

Then he made me hunch over in a wrestling stance. "Let me see you growl like this—*errrrrrrrrr!*"

And, amazingly, I did it!

He said, "Good! Good! I think we've got somethin' here!"

I said, "Well, let me think about it."

"Don't think too long because I can find other big funny guys!"

I told him, "Well, thank you, I appreciate it." And I escaped before he had the chance to show me how to make fake blood spurt from my ears.

■ ■ ■

But I finally did find a booking agent who would send me out to entertain groups like the Kiwanis and Knights of Columbus. He would often book me along with all kinds of old-time acts that had started in vaudeville. I remember one very elderly man who had a canine act featuring what he called his Gigantic Dogs. These were simply fat old dogs who were each about fifty pounds overweight. He would always end his show with the proclamation: "Folks, if you tell other people how good the show was—ATTENDANCE WILL MOUNT!" With that, one dog was supposed to mount another one and start humping. This would be the lingering image left with the uniformly repulsed audience. Then I would go on and try to obliterate the memory.

What I enjoyed most was the fact that the dogs were not exactly sharp and they regularly missed cues. More often than not, the old man would have to yell three or four times, "ATTENDANCE WILL MOUNT!" And the dogs would look around dazed. So he'd just keep repeating, "ATTENDANCE WILL MOUNT!" People in the audience would turn to each other, muttering, "What is he talking about?"

The only thing that ever really mounted was the level of discomfort in the room.

■ ■ ■

I found another way to get the chance to perform in front of audiences: Bribery! I'd quickly learned that comedy didn't exactly fit with most entertainment policies of the era. The coffeehouses preferred their angry folk singers and poets who hated their parents. Which was fine. So I decided to bypass those places and seek out bars and taverns that happened to have stages. Wherever I went, I carried a fifty-dollar bill. I'd go into a place, find the manager or bartender, and lay the fifty down in front of him. Then I would make my pitch: "Can I go on your stage and tell some jokes? If I do badly and people walk out, you can keep the fifty. And if I do okay, just give me my fifty back." It seemed to work, because they'd usually let me go on. Even if I didn't get many laughs, they'd tell me afterward: "Look, kid, I don't want your money. Just don't show your face around here again!"

In fact, no one ever kept the money. So I always had the same fifty-dollar bill—a small point of pride. And, every now and then, I did well enough to be invited back.

One day, I made this proposition at a club called the Beachcomber in Revere Beach, Massachusetts. The manager didn't take the fifty. He just told me to come back that night and I could go on. Of course, I was thrilled. As I walked out, though, he hollered after me: "Just make sure you wear old clothes!"

I didn't quite understand. But I figured, I'm doing a gig; I might as well dress up. So I ignored him and put on my "Sunday-best" green woolen suit. When I got there, the guy said, "That's an old suit, right?"

"No, I wanted to wear something good."

He shook his head and said, "Well, just remember—I warned you."

Again I was mystified. But I went up onstage and started to do my act. Right away, it occurred to me that this was the smokiest club I'd ever seen. Thick clouds just hung over the room. It looked like a cancer convention. Moreover, people seemed to be smoking their cigarettes all the way down to the filters. Everywhere the orange embers flashed like fireflies. And I do mean fireflies. Because suddenly I saw one lit butt sail up toward the stage! Then another one! And another! People were actually flicking their cigarette butts in my direction! I kept telling my jokes, kind of dodging these little white missiles.

Then I heard a few people down front going, "HAR-HAR-HAR!" That's when I noticed a strange smell. Then I saw smoke coming from the shoulder of my jacket.

I screamed, "Aaahhh! I'm on fire!"

The audience was roaring. "HAR-HAR-HAR!"

I batted out the smoldering jacket, while other butts kept flying toward me. Now they were making contact. Repeatedly. And I was hollering, "Hey! Ow! Ow! Ow!"

Suddenly, I understood what the guy had meant about wearing old clothes. By the time I left the stage, my suit was dotted with black holes! It was as though I was put through some ancient Native American trial by fire!

The manager smiled at me as I came off and said, "I told you, didn't I?" Tough club.

■ ■ ■

My first real breakthrough came the day I met Lennie Sogoloff, who ran a renowned jazz club on U.S. Route 1, in Peabody, Massachusetts, called Lennie's on the Turnpike. To this day, whenever Lennie comes out to sit in the *Tonight Show* audience, I always tell the crowd, "This is the man who gave me my start . . . so if I'm lousy tonight, blame him!" His place was one of the last of its kind, where for $8.95 you got a prime rib dinner and saw a big-name act. But he always liked comedians—

and, more important, he liked me. I walked into his office one day and told him I wanted to be a comedian.

He said, "Okay, do your act for me right now. Make me laugh!"

So I stood in front of his desk and did about twenty minutes of material. He seemed impressed enough, because I suddenly became his house comic, making twenty-five dollars a night for two half-hour sets. I would open for such name acts as Mose Allison, America, Linda Ronstadt, Bette Midler, and Kris Kristofferson. (Ironically, Chuck Findley, who today plays trumpet in the *Tonight Show* band, was a fixture at Lennie's back then.)

What was most significant for me was that this was the first time I ever played to an audience that actually *listened*. When I went onstage, people would go, "Ssssshhhhhh," and give me their focus. Prior to that, at strip joints, I was just an annoyance who slowed the parade of naked women. And

Lennie's on the Turnpike, my first real nightclub gig.

the material that worked in those places—like Umpire, the hygiene spray For Men With Foul Balls—now seemed hopelessly dumb. It would just die. I realized how bad I was. At Lennie's, when a joke got laughs, I knew it had some kind of merit. More than anywhere else, I was learning how to gauge my act and how to be a comedian.

Of course, none of this held true in my very first appearance there.

After I did my little private audition for Lennie, he announced, "Hey, Buddy Rich is coming in Saturday. You open the show!" This was thrilling and terrifying all at once. Buddy Rich was the country's premier jazz drummer, and he attracted crowds of slick guys in sunglasses, who bopped and snapped fingers at their tables. I expected to face a challenge but not quite the nightmare that occurred.

That night, Lennie came onstage to introduce me. He said, "Okay, ladies and gentlemen, before I bring out Buddy, I've got a bright young comedian—"

"*Booooo! Booooo!*"

It had started that fast. One extremely big guy down front wanted no part of me.

"—so please give him your attention," Lennie continued. "Welcome Jay Leno!"

At which point, the guy in front screamed, "WE HATE HIM!"

I thought, "How can they hate me? I've never even been *anywhere* before! It's my first time and the man hates me!" I tried to rationalize: "Did he see me in traffic? Does he know my parents?"

But I took the stage and grabbed the mike: "Hey everybody, how you doing! Nice to see you! Hey, ever been to McDonald's—"

And this guy hollered, *"You better bring Buddy out, man!"*

I calmly said, "Well, Buddy is getting ready. He'll be out here in a few minutes. Hope you enjoy—"

"GET BUDDY OUT HERE! GET HIM OUT HERE RIGHT NOW!"

The people around him were now telling him, "Take it easy! Take it easy!"

So I tried to engage him: "Sir, how you doin' tonight?" And I reached out to shake his hand.

Big mistake. He stood up and, suddenly, BAM! He decked me. I hit the stage and saw birds. From the corner of my eye, I spotted Lennie pounding the stage and saying, "Get up! Get up!" Like I needed a cut man. "Get up! Get up!"

Meanwhile, the big guy in front was saying, "You get up, man, I'm gonna knock you down again!" His friends tried to pull him down into his seat. But he shook them off and kept screaming. "No, this idiot is gonna pay!"

I didn't know what to do! If I got up, this guy was going to kill me! And Lennie kept saying, "Get up! Get up!" Maybe he wanted me dead. The rest of the audience was buzzing: *"What's going on?"* *"Oh, the comic must have insulted that guy."*

Fine! Now it was *my fault!*

Somehow I did get up and finish my act. But all I could think was: "Maybe I should have listened to that wrestling manager."

6

BULLETS AND FRENCH-FRIED POTADAHS

Because Gene Braunstein graduated a year ahead of me, I had to get my own apartment. This place would eventually turn into kind of a legendary crash pad for other young comedians who came through Boston. And *crash* was truly the operative word. By the time I left, I didn't bother to ask for the security deposit back. It probably wouldn't have covered the damages, anyway. Especially after what Freddie Prinze did there. But I'll get to that in a bit.

I had moved just down the block from where Gene and I lived, to 1754 Commonwealth Avenue. I paid one hundred sixty dollars a month for a second-floor walk-up. One day, not long after I moved in, there was a knock at the door. A delivery guy said, "I've got a refrigerator for you!"

I said, "For me?"

He said, "Yeah, your landlord's giving you a new refrigerator."

I said, "Really? I didn't ask for one."

He said, "You want it or not?"

I shrugged and said, "Sure, fine. Put it right there. Are you going to take the old one?"

"No, we don't take old ones."

So I said that I'd get rid of it myself. A buddy of mine came over later and we managed to get it out onto the back porch. Right below my second-floor railing was a huge Dumpster. On a whim, we lifted the refrigerator and heaved it over the railing—and directly into the Dumpster, where it landed with a crash.

After a few days, there was another knock at the door. A loud, insistent knock. It was the lady who lived downstairs. She screamed, "You took my refrigerator!"

I said, "What are you talking about?"

"You're a thief!" And she pushed past me into the kitchen. "There it is! There it is! You stole my refrigerator!"

I said, "I didn't steal anything! The guy delivered it here and said I was getting a new refrigerator!"

"That's my refrigerator! I'm calling the landlord!"

I said, "Don't call anybody."

But she did and the landlord called me, screaming. I told him about the delivery guy. He said, "Well, he screwed up! Where's the old one?"

Uh-oh. I lied: "Oh, it's right next to the new one."

"Well, it better be there!"

And I thought, "Now I've got to get the old one out of the stupid Dumpster!" So I got a couple of buddies and we pulled out the old one, which by then was buried under a mountain of garbage. We hauled it back up into my kitchen and plugged it in. Amazingly, it still worked. But it now made a terrible high-pitched humming sound, not unlike a distant police siren.

And, worse, it walked! Every few hours, it would move itself far enough to yank the plug out of the wall! Apparently, the fall from the porch had knocked a pulley out of whack, and now the machine had gone insane. At night, you could hear it making rounds.

To keep it from roaming the kitchen, I tried to wedge tables and chairs against it. But the refrigerator just pushed them away. Eventually, I got wooden planks and built a restraining box around it, which looked awful but did the job. Of course, the terrible squealing never stopped. I always had to close the kitchen door just to hear the TV.

But there was still another embarrassing refrigerator incident: One day, I came out of my apartment and saw a refrigerator sitting on the curb, near the trash. Now, when you throw out a refrigerator, you're supposed to bust off the handle, so kids can't get trapped inside. This one still had a handle, which I thought was irresponsible of whoever was getting rid of it. So I went back up to my apartment for a hammer, then came down and smashed the inside catch and broke off the handle. Then, to be doubly safe, I knocked the hinges off the door. I was very proud of my good citizenship. I took the hammer back upstairs, then came down again. This time, I found a woman sobbing on the curb and saw a guy running up and down the street. He rushed over to me and asked breathlessly, "Hey! You live here?" I said that I did.

He said, "Nice neighborhood you live in!"

I said, "What do you mean?"

"Well, we're moving in and some asshole just smashed our refrigerator!"

I swallowed hard and said, "Uh, *I didn't see anybody!*"

The woman was moaning, "Why, oh, why did we move here?"

I said, "Well, we've never had any problems before. Um, maybe somebody thought you were throwing it away."

"Nobody throws away a brand-new refrigerator!"

I said, "Well, you're certainly right about that! I'll keep my eyes open!"

■ ■ ■

Here is the kind of god-awful mess I made of the apartment: I once decided to leave my Christmas tree up all year long. I wanted to see if it would last until the following Christmas. (This could be ascribed to my Scottish thriftiness, but I preferred to think of it as an endeavor launched in the name of *science*!) By the middle of January, of course, the tree had turned into a brown dried-out fire trap. For the next eleven months, needles plummeted to the floor. When Christmastime came again, I hung ornaments on naked twigs. It looked like the tree of the Crypt Keeper. And, thus, I proved a point, which somehow eludes me now.

I remember that my first winter in the apartment was freezing. I couldn't get any heat out of my radiator. Somebody must have tightened the valve, then painted over it, sealing it in place. It wouldn't budge. Finally, when I could see my breath indoors, I got out the pliers and went at the valve, twisting and turning furiously. The valve never moved, so I got a vise-grip and started pulling on the pipe in front—until it broke! Steam came hissing out from the hole I'd made—but, thankfully, the radiator was getting hot. The only problem was that there was no way to regulate it, much less shut it off again.

Now I had the opposite problem. The apartment was turning into a sauna. And the only way to stop it would be to shut off all the steam in the building—not a viable option. After a couple of sweltering days in the apartment, I was happy to leave town for a gig. The radiator was in the kitchen—so, to keep the heat to a minimum, I just closed the kitchen door before taking off.

Naturally, this was idiotic thinking. When I came back a few days later, all the kitchen cabinets had buckled. None of the drawers would open. Everything was bent and twisted. The door stuck on its wooden frame. Even the wood I'd nailed around the refrigerator had warped. And the refrigerator was still screaming! What I now had was a funhouse kitchen.

And then it just got worse.

■ ■ ■

I would meet other comics who would blow through town on the Playboy Club circuit and always offered to let them stay at the apartment. The idea was that they would return the favor whenever I came to New York for audition nights. Unknowns like Richard Lewis and Billy Crystal were among the guys who flopped at my place, in addition to other unknowns who have remained unknown. I can report that both Lewis and Crystal were well-behaved houseguests. But many others contributed to the ongoing trashing of the premises.

Which brings me to Freddie Prinze, a wild but wonderful kid of seventeen when we met. He had come up from the streets, but always kept a kind of sweet innocence about him. In fact, I taught him how to drive a car. Within two years, he would get his shot on *The Tonight Show*—December 6, 1974, to be exact (comedians not only remember the dates of their own first shots with Johnny Carson, but everyone else's, too). That appearance immediately got him the sitcom *Chico and the Man*, and enormous fame. The success turned out to be too much too soon for Freddie, which led to his tragic end.

Even when I first knew him, he was full of demons. His two greatest fascinations were guns and women. And it was probably over a woman that he sat on my couch one night while I was out, firing his gun at the wall between the living room and my bedroom. From what I could tell, he must have unloaded about two hundred rounds of live ammunition. The wall was left with a gaping hole, roughly the size of a small window. At the very least, it did improve cross-ventilation.

But I also remember one famous night at the Boston Playboy Club when Freddie was shot at by a guy in the audience. Freddie was a raw performer whose work tended toward the obscene, which was still fairly rare in those days. Every other word would be *suck*—or worse. That night, a guy at a table hollered up at him and said, "Hey! Can you take it easy! I've got my mom here!" Freddie ignored him and launched into a bit about President Nixon's sex life. This just further provoked the guy, who said, "Hey, will you show a little respect!"

Freddie just said, "You're right, buddy! Nixon doesn't fuck. He *sucks*!"

At which point, the guy pulled out a gun and began firing at the bandstand. Freddie dived for safety. People ran for the exits. Bunnies were shrieking in terror. Pandemonium broke loose. Police charged in and hauled the guy away. Freddie was the kind of exciting performer who made bulletproof vests a wise consideration for audiences.

By the time Freddie shot himself to death, most of the comedians in our peer group had moved to California. Naturally, we all wanted to go to his funeral. But his manager had put out word that he wanted "names only" at the service. We went, anyway. Of course, there's nothing worse than comedians at a funeral. Your tendency is to always make a joke. Probably for this reason, we had to sit in the back. Whereas Freddie's *close* friends like Lucille Ball and Tony Orlando were in the front pews. During Tony Orlando's eulogy, I glanced down the aisle and saw the comedian Gary Muledeer waving his parking stub, whispering loudly, *"Do they validate? Do they validate?"* We all tried to stifle our laughter, like a bunch of bad schoolboys.

There was one ironic twist: Freddie's funeral took place in the Burbank Forest Lawn Chapel, above the door of which was an engraved commemoration of the Revolutionary War. As we all walked in, we passed under the words: "The shot heard 'round the world."

■　■　■

After Lennie's on the Turnpike closed, I divided my time between New York open-mike nights and working the Playboy circuit, where I would open for up-and-coming singers. Sometimes I played to a lot of empty tables. I would start out with lines like, "I'm glad to welcome *both of you* to the Playboy Club!" Or: "Where are you chairs from?" The Playboy Clubs, of course, were not known for their fine food as much as for who served it. And even though the presence of Bunnies helped, the food was fairly awful. For instance, the clubs didn't have french fries—just shoestring potatoes from cans. At least the rooms were so dark, people couldn't see what they were eating.

One night, my parents came to see me perform. Of course, neither of them was comfortable around the scantily clad Bunnies, but my father was especially bothered by the darkness in the showroom. I had just begun my act when I heard the voice boom.

"I CAN'T SEE THE GOD-DAMN MENU!"

Then I heard my mother: "Shhhhh! Quiet, the boy's onstage!"

"WELL, HOW THE HELL ARE WE SUPPOSED TO ORDER FOOD IF WE CAN'T SEE THE MENU?"

By now, everyone was listening. Not to give away who he was, I said, "Hey, buddy, please—I'm doing my show."

He didn't even hear me. A Bunny came over to him with a little flashlight so he could see. Then he ordered: "LET ME HAVE THE STEAK AND THE FRENCH-FRIED POTADAHS!" Then that nightmare passed.

Thankfully, I was later robbed of all this jewelry!

Until ten minutes later when the food arrived. At which point, the entire room heard: "WHAT KIND OF POTADAHS ARE THESE?!"

The Bunny said meekly, "Well, those are the shoestring potatoes, sir."

"BUT I ORDERED THE FRENCH-FRIED POTADAHS!"

It was hopeless. I just stopped the act and said, "Hey, Dad! Will you keep it down, please? I'll get you some french fries on the way home! Just cut it out!"

■　■　■

Every performer had his or her own private hell. I witnessed all versions of hell at the Boston Playboy Club. But one stands out as unforgettably miserable. On Fridays and Saturdays, we would do six shows a night—half in the Playmate Room and the other half in the Playboy Room, which was directly upstairs. The house band was the Bob Winters Trio, and one weekend, the featured singer was a girl named Kathy Nixon. To keep the shows moving, she would go on first in the Playmate Room downstairs. Then I went on next, while she would go upstairs and open the show in the Playboy Room. Then when I finished, I would go up and close the show in the Playboy Room while she went back downstairs to start the next show.

That was bad enough. But that weekend, the drummer in the band was involved in some union dispute and wouldn't carry his own drums between the shows. So the job fell to this poor girl, Kathy Nixon, who lugged the full drum set up and down the two flights of stairs *six times a night*!

By the third show, she would have huge sweat stains under

her dress and her hair would be a mess. And I couldn't help her, because I'd be onstage! During my act, I'd hear the cymbals crashing against the banister and the snare drums tumbling down the steps. Then, invariably, I'd hear her sobbing on the staircase. I don't know if she's still in show business. If not, I suspect that she could have signed on with the Allied Van Lines people.

■ ■ ■

At the New York Playboy Club, they had a classically stupid way of making introductions. Every singer would be introduced with: "Make way for the *song stylings* of Miss Whomever!" For comedians like me, it was: "Here's a very funny gentleman who has *entertained the crowned heads of Europe!*" They did this, I suppose, because there'd be no way to check for substantiation. Nobody at any Playboy Club was ever going to know whether King Gustav had really rolled in the aisles of his palace. For that matter, nobody at any Playboy Club had probably ever *heard* of King Gustav.

It was always more important for *one particular person* at the Playboy Club to enjoy your act. This was the room director, usually a guy named Vinnie or Tony, who was the kind of show business sage who had graduated from the ranks of busboy. The room director would grade the acts after every show in a report card that "would be seen by Mr. Hefner himself!" (As though a man running a vast empire would care how the comic did in his 8:45 set in Lake Geneva, Wisconsin.) Sillier still, you would have to sign the report card after you had been graded. At least you didn't have to show it to your parents.

Anyway, one Saturday night, I came into the New York

club to do the first show as usual. I would follow a singer, who seemed to do well enough to win great applause.

Then I came on, facing what I thought was an audience like any other. I started: "Hey, everybody! How you doin'?" They all just blankly stared at me and smiled a little. I figured this was a tough crowd, so I just kept plowing forward. They kept smiling except for two people in front who politely laughed.

After my first five minutes, most of them had begun talking among themselves. This was terrible. I picked out one guy in the audience and asked, "How are you tonight, sir? What do you do for a living?" The guy just smiled at me and nodded. I couldn't understand what was happening.

Now I was dying a horrible death, sweating through my clothes. I tried the McDonald's material. Nothing. The growing-up-in-New-England stuff. Nothing. Stories about my parents. (*Everybody has parents!*) Just nothing. I finished and left the stage to a quiet smattering of applause.

The room director was waiting for me, arms folded, grim look on his face.

"Hey, come here!" he said, flashing my report card. "Man, you get an F!"

He scrawls on the card, "F! Comic stunk!" Then he handed it to me and said, "Here! Sign that!"

I said, "Come on, this is an impossible crowd!"

Then the maitre d' ran over and said, "Hey, don't blame the kid! They're all foreigners! They're all from Portugal!"

I said, "Portugal? They don't speak English?"

The maitre d' said, "No, the whole room was all foreigners!"

Nobody bothered to tell me that two hundred Portuguese

tourists on a New York weekend package had descended on the Playboy Club for bad steaks and a comedian they couldn't understand. The only two people who laughed turned out to be translators!

The room director's arms were still folded. He grunted at me and said, "So you could have done some Portuguese stuff! You could have made the people in your jokes come from Portugal! You still get an F!"

I said, "*I didn't know they were Portuguese!* You can't give me an F!"

"Are you gonna sign the card?"

"I'm not signing it!"

"Hey, you don't sign it, you don't do the next two shows! Also, you don't get paid! *And Mr. Hefner's gonna see this!*"

I signed it. But, after that night, I did come up with a new foolproof greeting line to start my act. In fact, these were the first words I spoke in my *Tonight Show* standup debut a few years later:

"I'm from the United States! Any United States people here tonight?"

By the way, I'm still waiting to hear from Hef.

▪ ▪ ▪

Show business is a world of hyperbole. Sometimes you have to trust your instincts in search of the truth. I remember playing Lowell State College, opening for a rock group called Kiva. That's pronounced KEE-va. I give you the pronunciation because, doubtless, you've never heard of them. I hadn't. Kiva consisted of two guys with long straight hair who looked like Nelson—the recent duo whose father was Ricky Nelson. The audience at Lowell didn't seem especially familiar with Kiva, but they gave polite ovations. Anyway, after the college gig, I got a call from Kiva's manager, who had a proposition to make.

He said, "Look, we'd like you to tour with Kiva. It'll be an all-encompassing nationwide tour. Before you answer, let me tell you a few things: A reporter from *Rolling Stone* will be traveling with Kiva to write an upcoming cover story. Also, along the way, a writer from *Time* magazine will be joining us to do a major feature, which will run when the tour winds up next year this time at the Forum in Los Angeles."

Now, as far as I knew, Kiva didn't even have an album out yet. I said, "Well, sounds great! What kind of money are you talking about?"

The manager said, "Well, we're not really talking about a *lot* of money."

I said, "Well, how much *are* we talking about?"

"We're talking about forty-five dollars a show."

I remembered advice someone had once given me: Never say no to a date. But when you don't want to do something, just set your price high. This way people won't be insulted.

So I told the guy, "Well, that's a little low. For something like that I'd usually get"—and I just made up a completely outlandish figure—"five *thousand* dollars a show."

There was a long pause. Then he said, "Well, we could *dicker . . .*"

I said, "*Really*? How are we gonna dicker? Are you going to come up to like fifty dollars and I'll come down to forty-nine hundred? You'll come up to seventy-five; I'll come down to forty-eight hundred?"

Suffice it to say, I didn't end up playing the big tour. As far as I recall, I don't think Kiva ever got their *Rolling Stone* and *Time* magazine covers, either. Maybe they're still dickering.

■ ■ ■

In Boston, I had a brief run of bad luck with thieves. My '54 Hudson Hornet was stolen one night, leaving me without wheels for a while. So I would hitchhike to gigs. One day, I was hitching a ride to play at a coffeehouse near Boston University. I'd barely stuck out my thumb on the Beacon Street Bridge over the Charles River, when a '65 Barracuda pulled up. Two guys were in the front seat and another guy was in back. The door opened and I got in the back. The guys all seemed a little panicky. One in front shot me a wild-eyed look and said, "Do you know what kind of car this is?"

Figuring that I would impress them with my automotive knowledge, I shrugged and said, "Yeah, it's a '65 Barracuda. And I believe it has the 270 V8 and the torque-flight automatic transmission."

At which point, the guy sitting next to me—who was also fairly scary-looking—took out a big hunting knife and held it to my throat. The guy in front now turned around and pointed a gun at me. He said, "It's too bad you know what kind of car this is. Now we'll have to kill you."

Clearly, I had gotten into the wrong car.

I said, "Well, I didn't see your license plate number or anything."

The guy with the gun said, "How much money you got?"

I said, "About seventy bucks, I guess."

"Give us the money! Give us your wallet!"

I said, "There's nothing in my wallet except my license."

He grabbed the money and said, "What about your boots? We'll take your boots!"

I said, "Look, why don't I just get out and I won't look at the car or anything. I'll lie down on the ground, whatever you want, and you can drive away."

This seemed agreeable to them. So they pulled over and I lay down on the ground until they peeled away. Somehow I still had my boots, but they had my money. I started walking to the gig, stopping off first at the police station to file a report. An officer took down all the information, gave me a long look, then said, "I'll have your seventy bucks back for you tonight."

I said, "Really? You know who these guys are?"

He said, "No, no. But I know how you can get your seventy bucks back."

I said, "Well, how?"

He said, "Where do you live?" I told him. "You gonna be home tonight?"

"Well, I have a gig tonight, I'll be home late."

"What time?"

I said, "Midnight."

"Okay. I'll come over at midnight."

I said, "And you're gonna have my seventy dollars?"

He gave an impatient sigh and said, "I have a way you'll get your seventy dollars back. Do you want it or not?"

For some reason, this cop was getting annoyed, so I said yes. After my gig, I was home by midnight when I heard knocking on the door. The cop came in, wearing street clothes and carrying a small suitcase. He put the suitcase on a table and said, "Okay, I'm going to tell you how to get your seventy bucks back."

"You mean you found those guys?"

"We're not gonna find those guys! We have no idea who they are! Will you just listen, please?" He opened up his case, one half of which was a record player. He took out a cardboard record and put it on the turntable. Then he said, "I'm gonna help you get your money back by selling Echo Silverware!"

I said, "What are you talking about?"

He said, "Do you want your money back or what? You're wasting my time."

I said, "All right, all right." He was a cop, after all.

He said, "Just listen to this." Then he played the record, which extolled the exciting benefits of selling Echo Silverware. When the record stopped, he said, "If I sign you up to sell this door-to-door, then you can sign up some other people, and— with your commissions—you can make seventy dollars in three days!"

"I don't really want to sell Echo Silverware."

"Well," he yelled, "*what are you wasting my time for?*"

I said, "I'm not wasting your time! You said you'd get me my money back!"

"*You're not gonna get your money back!* You're being unreasonable! Here I'm showing you how you can get your money back and *you're not interested!*" Now he pulled out all kinds of brochures and flatware samples and laid them in front of me. "This is all you need to make money!"

I finally said, "Well, can I think about it and let you know?"

"You're not interested, are you?"

I said, "Well, no."

"*Then what are you doing wasting my time?*"

"*Your* time! You're wasting *my* time!"

He just glowered at me and said, "Hey, do you want me to run you in right now?"

I was robbed and now he was threatening to arrest me for my reckless indifference to flatware! If I had my seventy bucks back, I guess I could've bought a couple of place settings to appease him. The seed of crime does bear some peculiar fruit.

7

A GOOD DOG WILL RUN TILL HIS HEART EXPLODES

B esides comedy, the only thing that ever really interested me was cars. The day I got my first apartment on Commonwealth, I remember noticing a car dealership down the street called Foreign Motors, which sold Rolls-Royces, Mercedes-Benzes, and Citroën SMs. Having already worked at Wilmington Ford and learned all the wonders of Falcons and Galaxies, I saw this as an opportunity for me to move up! So the day after I unpacked, I walked over and asked for a job. The sales manager, Seldon Loring, said he didn't need anybody. I left, but not before getting a glimpse of the bay where the new cars were cleaned and prepped for buyers. The next day, I went back and just started working with the prep guys. I told them, "I'm new here. What do you want me to do?" (I used to tell a joke about prepping new cars: I'd say I was the guy whose job it was to smear the grease stains under the paper floor mats.)

A couple of days passed before Seldon Loring caught sight of me. He said, "What are you doing here?"

I said, "Oh, I've just been working here for a couple of days."

"Who hired you?"

"Um, nobody."

Then some of the prep guys told him, "Hey, he's been doing a good job!" Which was all it took. Since he was a car salesman, I think he appreciated this kind of chutzpah; he hired me on the spot. Because I was a college student and fairly glib, the bosses would elect me to do the odd errand and inter-face with customers. I was the one who drove customers home when they brought cars in for servicing. And I also got to deliver the new Rolls-Royces and Mercedeses to buyers' homes. Of course, these were some of the richest people in Boston.

Arthur Fiedler, the legendary Boston Pops conductor, would have his car brought in from time to time. Strange as it sounds, he was fascinated with the fire department. So, when-ever a fire broke out and he was without a car, I'd be told, "Jay, go pick up Arthur Fiedler and take him to the fire!" I'd pull up to his house and he would jump in the car, saying, "There's a fire in Roxbury!" And we'd race to the scene so he could watch the leaping flames. His eyes would sparkle like a little kid's. Eventually, the fire department gave him a siren and flashing lights for his red Mercedes.

Another task that fell to me was driving the recipients of Harvard's Hasty Pudding awards to the ceremony each year. Because they were visiting celebrities, Harvard wanted them ferried around in style. I drove for Liza Minnelli and Faye Dunaway, among others. One year, John Wayne was given the award, and instead of a limousine, he was taken to the event in an army tank. My job was to follow him in a Rolls-Royce in case anything went wrong. Nothing did, except for the moment after his speech, when he asked the audience for questions. Harvard, of course, was a hotbed of radicalism and liberal thinking. So a woman got up and asked him, "What do you think of women's liberation?"

John Wayne swaggered as only he could and said, "I think women's lib is fine, as long as they're home by six to cook my dinner."

The crowd gave a thunderous cheer. But the woman was furious and she shrieked, "Fuck you, John Wayne!"

And he just swaggered again and said, "Well, fuck you, too, little lady!"

He got a huge laugh. But I think he needed that tank to get out of there.

My favorite Hasty Pudding winner was Jack Lemmon, whom I picked up at the airport. He was very nice to me. We got to talking and I told him I wanted to be a comedian. He gave me a big smile and said, "Well, maybe we'll be neighbors in Beverly Hills someday!" The best part of this story is that now we actually *are* next-door neighbors in Beverly Hills. I think that was what made me buy the house I live in. I get to wave to Jack Lemmon on my way to work every day. Sometimes he even waves back.

■ ■ ■

There were other benefits of the job. One night, I had to deliver Joseph Kennedy's 1954 Rolls-Royce Silver Wraith limousine somewhere. I stopped off and picked up my girlfriend, then drove to a secluded lovers' lane area, where we made love. Made love . . . *in the backseat of Joseph Kennedy's*

Silver Wraith! We were parked next to rows of Volkswagens where other couples were cramped and contorted and probably sustaining concussions. We just pulled down the shades in the back windows and sprawled out in what I would fondly remember as the Hyannisport Sexmobile. Eventually, some of the people came over from their Volkswagens to ask me about the car. I told them it belonged to Old Man Kennedy. They asked who I was. Thinking fast, I told them that I was *Larry* Kennedy, the brother nobody ever talks about.

Often I would sort of "borrow" the occasional Rolls or Mercedes for a night. Gene Braunstein and I would then cruise around town trying to impress college girls. We came up with a scam in which I rode in the backseat and Gene drove. At the time, because of my long hair and little glasses, I bore a vague resemblance to the English pop star Donovan. So we would pull up next to girls on the street and I'd lower the window. Invariably, they would say, "Hey, isn't that Donovan?" Gene

A bad hair day.

would say, "Yes, it is—and I'm his manager. Would you like to meet him?" Girls would climb into the backseat and I would have my British accent down perfectly: "Hullo there, I'm Donovan! 'Ow are ya, luv?" Worked like a charm. I wonder if Donovan will ever know how well he did for himself in Boston during the early seventies.

■　■　■

Some nights after work, I was sent to pick up cars at the Rolls-Royce headquarters in Paramus, New Jersey, on Route 15. And, although I wasn't supposed to do it, I always drove from there into New York to try to get on at The Improv. Every night I would pull up in a different new Rolls or Mercedes, which would create a big stir. Budd Friedman, who owns The Improv, was convinced that I was some ridiculously wealthy young comedian—an impression that I enjoyed giving. He had no idea that I was driving in from Boston every night. He just thought I was the son of an influential New York capitalist with a massive car collection. This might have been the reason he was so nice to me and always gave me a spot onstage.

One night I picked up a Rolls in Paramus, then delivered it to a customer who lived nearby. He paid me twenty-nine thousand five hundred dollars in cash, which he handed over in a brown paper lunch sack. I went back to Paramus to pick up another Rolls, then raced to The Improv to try to go on for a set. I got there by midnight and, as usual, parked the Rolls on the street near Forty-fourth and Ninth where the club resided.

But I still had the twenty-nine grand and figured I'd better not leave it in the car. So I brought it inside, clutching it like it was my lunch. Budd told me that I could go on at around one-thirty, so I just held the bag until it was my turn.

Finally, I went onstage and set the bag on the piano behind me. Because I was going to try out some new material that night, I also had my little tape recorder, which I placed near the bag and switched on. That way I could listen back later and gauge how well the stuff went over. As it turned out, there weren't more than twenty people in the audience, but the new jokes were killing them! It was one of the best receptions I'd ever gotten, which just pumps you with amazing amounts of adrenaline. By the time I finished, I was flying high.

So I grabbed the tape recorder, ran out to the Rolls, and drove off feeling exhilarated. As I sped along, I listened to the tape and heard all those laughs I'd gotten over and over again. I had just gone through the tollbooth in Greenwich, Connecticut, when it hit me: *I didn't have the twenty-nine grand!* I'd left it on top of the piano! By now, some comic was probably spending it on hookers!

Like a maniac, I turned around and tore back to New York. At this point, it was almost four in the morning and The Improv was about to close. I burst inside and saw a girl singing onstage. Behind her was the piano and on the piano—unbelievably!—was the brown paper bag. So I sneaked up onstage and the girl shot me an angry look. I pointed to the bag and whispered, "I forgot my lunch! Sorry!"

I looked inside and, thank God, saw that the huge wad was still there. It was my luckiest night in show business! Because I've always thought: Had it been gone, I would literally just be getting out of jail now! My whole career never would have happened!

▪ ▪ ▪

The first night I ever auditioned at The Improv, Freddie Prinze auditioned, too. And so did a comedian named Steve Lubetkin, who later also met an infamous fate when he leaped off the roof of the Hyatt Hotel on Sunset Boulevard, next door to The Comedy Store. Early on, I began to see a trend in comedians who eventually self-destructed. In most such cases, they were guys trying to use standup as a steppingstone for an acting career. They often made the mistake of assuming that doing comedy would be the easiest part of the progression. They didn't find enough joy in just telling the jokes. Also, they often neglected to put themselves in the place of the audience. They heard only their own voices, ignoring the response of the crowd. Countless times, I'd watch someone get virtually no laughs, then ask him afterward how he thought he'd done. And invariably the answer would be, "Oh, I *killed!*" This phe-nomenon is called *laugh ears*—the delusion that you hear laughs when, in fact, there are none.

I always believed that being a comic required a certain tenacity, which I was lucky enough to have. To audition at places like Catch a Rising Star and The Improv, we would start lining up outside the clubs at two in the afternoon with hopes of getting onstage sometime after eleven that night. You'd spend your whole day sitting on the curb, waiting and waiting. Inevitably, somebody in front of you would say, "This sucks!" and walk away. I always enjoyed that. All of a sudden, I had moved up! Without my doing a thing, my standing in show business had just improved! And that process seemed to encompass my philosophy of life.

That's why I originally wanted to call this book *A Good*

Dog Will Run Till His Heart Explodes—an old hunting expression that I've always loved. When I was a child, one image was drilled into my head and has stayed with me ever since: While I was goofing off or watching TV, Russian kids were studying math. I don't know if that was true, but it sounded intimidating. So I chose to believe that whenever I was doing nothing, someone else was catching up and taking everything I had. (This is what still makes vacations agony for me.)

The point is, any idiot can have a life. If you're breathing, you've got a life. But careers are hard to come by. I've never been better at anything than anybody else. Which meant that I would always just have to work a little harder to keep up or maybe even pull ahead. Like the turtle who raced the hare, I plowed forward, slow and steady. Even if it meant sitting on curbs all day or sleeping on the back steps of comedy clubs all night.

In fact, I have vivid memories of sleeping in the alley next to The Improv. If there was no place to crash and I was too tired to drive back to Boston, I would hunker down against the brick wall near Dyke's Lumberyard and try to doze off. I soon learned that prostitutes liked to bring guys into the same alley. Some nights I'd wake up to the sounds of sleazy sales pitches or low moaning or, worse, somebody getting slapped. I would cower there and feel like Dustin Hoffman in *Midnight Cowboy*. (Ironically, Dustin Hoffman was once the house piano player at The Improv. I think he must have researched Ratso Rizzo in that alley.)

■ ■ ■

Spontaneous bedlam occasionally broke out at The Improv. There was a nearby strip joint called Broadway Burlesque, and sometimes girls who worked there would come in after work. After a few cocktails, they liked to amuse themselves by taking off their clothes again in our club. Naturally, this also amused all the comedians present. One night, during my act, I needed somebody to come onstage to help me do a bit. I picked a young woman in the front row. I didn't realize until later that she had just gotten off work at Broadway Burlesque. I just knew that whenever I looked away from her, the audience would roar with laughter. I'd think, "It can't be me!" I hadn't said anything funny yet. Then I found out that she had been flashing the crowd behind my back.

On another night, when I was working as emcee, one woman came onstage totally naked. The crowd went batty. Budd Friedman ran around locking doors to prevent a vice raid. Then another girl screamed, "Her body's terrible!" Whereupon she took her clothes off, as if to challenge the first naked woman. Suddenly, everybody in the club was undressing, partially or completely. I think I ended up in my underwear, which seemed to have a sobering effect on the room. But then you've always got to leave them wanting more.

■ ■ ■

Because there was no money to be made in the open-mike clubs, comedians were often paid with food. I learned that there was a pecking order in most of these places. As one club owner explained it: The opening act could have any of the sandwiches from the vending machine out back. The middle act could have any of the appetizers on the menu. And the headliner could have any of the entrées, except steak or roast beef. When I headlined for that owner, I once asked: "Can I give the opening act my potatoes?" He looked stricken and said, "No, you can't do that! There's no sharing! If you do it, then everybody's gonna give the opening act their potatoes! You'll ruin it for everyone!"

At The Improv, I always loved to emcee, because Budd gave me free-run of the menu. One night, I ate five sirloin steaks. Which quickly put an end to my free-run of the menu. But some people had a hard time understanding these cryptic club policies. For instance, early on in my Improv days, my father asked me, "How's the comedy thing going?"

"Good, Pop, good. I'm down in New York a lot."

"What's that nightclub you play at? The Improv? What's the fellow pay you down there?"

"Nothing."

"What do you mean *nothing?*"

"He doesn't pay *anybody*, Dad."

"He charges people to get in?"

"Yeah."

"He charges for the drinks?"

"Yeah."

"WHAT THE HELL IS THAT? HE'S MAKING MONEY OFF OF YOU! YOU TELL HIM YOUR FATHER SAYS YOU SHOULD GET A COUPLE OF BUCKS!"

I said, "No, Dad, I'm not gonna tell him that."

"THEN I'M GONNA GET THAT SON OF A BITCH ON THE PHONE! YOU'RE NOT WORKING FOR FREE!"

"Dad, you're not gonna call him on the phone! It's show business! It's the way it works! You go down and you work for free!"

"HE'S TAKING ADVANTAGE OF YOU!"

I suppose he had a point, but that was how it worked. That, however, was probably the night I ate the five steaks.

■ ■ ■

The most exciting rite of passage to witness was whenever a comedian whom we knew got a shot on national television. This was an amazing phenomenon—to actually *know* somebody on TV! One by one, we saw guys go forth and do it. The great neurotic comic Richard Lewis was the first from our graduating class, so to speak, to make the cut. (By then, I had already been in awe of Lewis. On my first night at The Improv, I'd seen a copy of the *Bergen County News* with a story about "local comic Richard Lewis." Then I turned around and actually met Lewis. I couldn't get over this! I was practically starstruck.)

Very early on, Lewis had done a *Tonight Show*, after which he came back to New York to wait for the next big break. Which came shortly thereafter. In those days, TV variety show producers would come to The Improv to scout talent. Sonny Bono, who was running *The Sonny & Cher Comedy Hour*, dropped in all the time. And one night, he must have spotted Lewis. The next thing we knew, they were flying Lewis to California to do the show. This was unbelievable! One of our own was going to do his act on prime-time TV! And, of course, mixed in with a bit of natural envy, we all were rooting for him.

Lewis called from out there to tell us when the show would air. So, that night, all the comics collected down at The Improv, where we huddled at the bar to watch the show at eight o'clock. Everybody fell quiet, waiting for Rich's shot. At some point, Sonny and Cher were involved in a sketch set in a vegetable garden. We were half paying attention, when suddenly we spotted Lewis dance by in the background, dressed as a lettuce leaf! Another guy was a carrot. Human vegetables were now spinning all over the place. We were stunned—and we were also on the floor laughing. Knowing Lewis, we knew he had to be humiliated. Rather than showing off his crackling urban wit, he had been reduced to a twirling piece of salad greens!

We called him right away, passing the phone around, saying things like, "Hey, great shot!" "You made us believe that lettuce could dance!" "Green is your color, man!" Strangely enough, vegetable or not, it was still very exciting.

■ ■ ■

Of any of us, Andy Kaufman was by far the most innovative comedian at that time—although he never liked being called a comedian. Clearly, his was the oddest act. Most of us thought he was very funny, but we worried that no one else would get him. We even sort of felt sorry for him, because he was so untraditional. (Of course, his great success proved us wrong.) Still, he never told any jokes. He just behaved strangely, in order to get a reaction of any kind, even hostile. There were nights at Catch a Rising Star when he would lie onstage in a sleeping bag. Other nights, he would read endless passages from *The Great Gatsby* in a monotonous voice. Or he would become the Foreign Man character, who spoke flurries of gibberish before turning into Elvis Presley—doing an astonishingly accurate impersonation.

At that time, shocking though it may seem now, I also did

an Elvis bit, in which I'd sneer a lot and sing Shakespearean soliloquies as the King might have. I also sung Lou Christie falsettos. Then, thankfully, my voice changed. But Andy and I enjoyed our Elvis kinship. (Years later, Dick Clark told me that he'd heard that Elvis himself was a fan of only two Elvis imper-sonations: Andy's and mine!) As it turned out, Andy was also commuting to New York from Boston, where he, too, attended college. So he often ended up driving down with me, although I can't say that I got to know him very well. With Andy, you never knew whom you were talking to. He liked to disappear into different personas offstage as well as onstage and refused to ever break character.

One character he liked to become was a very sleazy,

Me doing a scene from an Elvis movie: "Hey, busboy, sing me a song!"

obnoxious lounge singer named Tony Clifton. Tony was Andy's alter ego, just a horrible person who demeaned audiences that hated him in return. As Tony, he would hide beneath layers of grotesque makeup and an enormous bad toupee and mustache. And he would never acknowledge that he was Andy Kaufman.

I would always approach him and say, "Hey, Andy!"

He would glower back and say, "I don't know who Andy is! He's been using my name to get places!"

As a small point of pride, I may have been the only person who ever got him to drop character. One day, I decided to appeal to him in a way that would provoke any comedian: I told him that somebody stole his act. I said, "Hey, Tony, when you see Andy, tell him I saw a guy last night at another club doing the whole Tony Clifton bit! Same mean-spirited bad singing—everything! It was unbelievable."

Suddenly, Tony's eyes turned into Andy's eyes, and they were full of panic.

Then, from under the makeup, I heard Andy Kaufman say, *"What guy? Where did you see this?"*

I cracked up: "Aha! Gotcha, Andy!"

I think he then tried to explain that he actually *was* Tony, doing an impersonation of Andy, even though he said he still had no idea who Andy was. He was a remarkable guy, but basically confusing to spend any time around.

■ ■ ■

Cruise directors for the big ocean-liner companies often turned up at The Improv, recruiting comedians as if we were rogue sailors. We were being shanghaied! They'd come in and holler, "I've got a three-day cruise to nowhere! All passengers from Long Island. Job pays seventy-five dollars for two shows, plus accommodations! Who wants it?"

And all the comics would scramble for the job!

It was like a bad-movie scene: Comedians waved their hands in the air, desperate to go seafaring. The cruise guy would survey the room, then say, "I'll pick two men! I'll take *that man* . . . and . . . *that one!*" The chosen ones would disappear for days, then return with tales of free food and Club Med girls they dated. It all sounded quite exotic. But I confess that I was always a tad leery of cruise gigs. The notion of being trapped with the audience for days at sea horrified me: If you did well, four hundred people would be patting you on the back all week. But if you did poorly, the passengers would hate you and let you know it whenever they saw you.

I was tempted only once.

One day, a cruise director showed up with an interesting proposition. He announced, "I've got a cruise. Four days to the Caribbean. I need a good comic!" I guess he had seen my act and liked it, because he approached me first. He said, "Why don't you take this job? Boat leaves Saturday and the pay is five hundred dollars for two shows!"

"Five hundred dollars!"

This was considerably more than the usual seventy-five bucks everybody else got. Unfortunately, that Saturday I was booked at a small upstate gig that paid only fifty dollars. But I thought it would be unprofessional to cancel on short notice. Still, I was intrigued.

I said, "Well, I don't know. I've got this thing . . ."

"I'm talking *five hundred dollars!*"

"I know! But how come this one pays so much more?"

"Different kind of cruise! A different group. They've got more money."

"What group is it?"

"I don't know! You want it or not?"

I did, but just couldn't. Dismayed by my own principles, I told him, "Well, I can't. I can't get out of this gig . . ."

"All right, the hell with you! I'll get somebody else!"

So the cruise guy went over to another comic, who instantly agreed to go. I don't remember his name, but I believe he never worked again after this job. I'll never forget the story he told when he returned:

Upon boarding ship, he went directly to his stateroom and fell asleep. About two hours out of port, he woke to the sounds of wild laughter on deck. He looked out the porthole and saw a naked guy run past. This was alarming enough. Then there was a knock at his cabin door. There stood another completely naked man, who told him, "Your showtime is in an hour."

The comic was stunned. He asked, "What's going on here? You're *naked*!"

The naked guy said, "Oh, didn't they tell you? This is a gay nude cruise and you're the entertainment!"

By now, the comic feared for his life. Fully dressed, he left his stateroom and walked along the deck, which was populated with hundreds of drunken naked men, frolicking and playing volleyball and sipping tropical drinks. Somehow he got to the stage to do his act. Before he could open his mouth, the all-naked crowd screamed, "Take your clothes off! Take 'em off!"

I don't know if he kept his clothes on. All he told us was that he locked himself in his stateroom until the ship returned to port. For the rest of the cruise, nude guys would bang on his door at all hours, bellowing, "Hey, *comedian!* Come on out here and *get naked! Wooooooooooo!*" I heard that he immediately spent his five hundred dollars on therapy.

■ ■ ■

I once got sucked into a nightmare in a similar fashion. A pharmaceutical entrepreneur came to The Improv in search of a comic to entertain potential buyers. I was the comic he selected. He told me that he was assembling a conference room full of Liggett-Rexall dealers in a midtown hotel, where he would introduce a new product. Sounded simple enough and the pay was seventy-five bucks, which was even better. But he somehow neglected to tell me what the product was—and I wasn't especially interested in finding out.

On the appointed day, I went to the hotel function room where about sixty area Liggett-Rexall dealers awaited the sales spiel. But first the entrepreneur took me aside and said, "I've got an idea: You pretend to be Bob Johnson, my director of sales. Just talk for a few minutes and then go into your comedy routine. Then, when they're all laughing, I'll stand up and tell them who you really are." Fine with me.

So then he started the proceedings: "Ladies and gentlemen, I have an exciting new product that will change the habits of American hygiene! The product is called Fresh'n, which we've imported from Japan. Fresh'n is a soft, moist towelette on a roll that should be used after bowel movements to *avoid embarrassing rectal odor!*"

The crowd immediately began to shift uncomfortably.

"Fresh'n is already a sensation in Japan," he continued,

"and I know you'll see it become a staple in every bathroom here! But before I show you the product, let me introduce you to my director of sales, Bob Johnson! Bob, come on out here and talk to these nice people!"

I stepped into the lion's den. The Rexall people were already appalled. I could see them squirming in their seats, itching to leave before another mention of Fresh'n could be made. I had neither the material nor the experience to distract them from the horror. But it was a gig, so I tried.

"Hi, my name is Bob Johnson, director of sales. I hope you all enjoy the product!" Nothing else to say. Certainly not about rectal odor. This was the first I'd heard of it! So I just launched into the act, which somehow now seemed incongruous: "Hey, have you ever been to McDonald's?" And so on. The Rexall people stared numbly and squirmed in silence. Death! I was supposed to be on for a half-hour, but since there were virtually no pauses for laughter, I was finished in fifteen minutes.

I sat down to no applause. The pharmaceutical guy quickly took the microphone, sweating bullets. He said, "That was not Bob Johnson, director of sales, of course—but Jay Leno, a *professional comedian*!" He applauded as if to start a wave, which never came. A Rexall guy down front muttered, "Yeah, he's a real professional, all right . . ."

He pushed on with the pitch: "So! Now who wants to be the first to sign up for Fresh'n? I'm going to do something rare here: If you take the first hundred cases, I'll throw in a case of Fresh'n *free* for yourself and your family! Whaddaya think of that?"

No one uttered a word. Perspiration poured off the guy.

"Well, let me show you the product!"

Now the crowd looked terrified, thinking that he was about to give an actual demonstration on the spot. He took out a Fresh'n sample, which was basically a big, wet roll of toilet paper, mounted on a plastic holder that adhered to the bathroom wall with stickum.

"You place the holder right beside the regular toilet paper dispenser where it can easily be reached. That way, it becomes second nature to wipe the rectal area once business is done!"

This was the most awful thing I'd ever seen. People were now getting up and leaving. He caught one guy and began to plead: "Sir! I'll tell you what! Just take a case home! Try it with the family! Believe me, I think they're gonna love it!"

The guy shook loose and said, "No, thanks!"

The unspoken presumption, of course, was that everyone in the room experienced embarrassing rectal odor. I guess it was a little too insulting to bear. Because, suddenly, half the people there were bolting.

At this point, the man who hired me actually began to cry. He whined, "*Look, I beg of you: I have three hundred thousand* cases of this stuff in my warehouse! Please, just take it! Just try it! Try it in your store! I've invested my whole life savings in this! Just see if you like it! Believe me, the people will come back!"

This had gotten more embarrassing than rectal odor. Now everyone had gotten up to leave. Suddenly, I was alone with the guy, who was hunched over, sobbing to himself, head cradled in his arms. Finally, I walked over and tapped him on the shoulder to ask for my seventy-five dollars.

He looked up at me, tears covering his face, and snapped,

"*Get outta here!* You *professional* comedian! You *ruined* my whole presentation! You got no laughs! You get no money! Get out! Just leave me alone!"

The man was so upset, I didn't really want to argue with him. So I just said, "Gee, I'm sorry it didn't work out, but I did what you told me to do. It's only seventy-five bucks . . ."

He gave me a disgusted look and grunted, "Look, just take a case of Fresh'n, if you want!"

Which I did. I took what I thought was about seventy-five dollars' worth of moist rectal towelettes. Not exactly a dream barter, but, hey, a deal's a deal.

8

BIG-TIME SHOW BUSINESS IN STUDY HALL C

During college, I was burning the candle at both ends and then some. Even while I was running around doing comedy, I kept my job at Foreign Motors. I would always put the money I made there in the bank, then use whatever money I made at comedy gigs for spending. By the time I got out of school, though, the comedy money had begun to exceed the day-job money. That's when I decided, "Well, let me give it a shot." And I became a full-time comedian.

Shortly before that pivotal time, I was still working the Playboy circuit. I remember getting a gig at the Cincinnati Playboy Club, for which I would make four hundred dollars in a weekend. The problem was that the airfare from Boston was four hundred fifty dollars round-trip. So I had to dip into my Foreign Motors money to get there, then pay for whatever lodging I could find on top. That weekend, I chose the Hotel Cincinnatian, which was then a dilapidated men's hotel—and has since been completely refurbished into one of the town's finest luxury hotels. Back then, it was three bucks a night; five bucks if you wanted a TV in your room. I took a TV room, but the TV had no antenna. So a guy at the front desk brought up a wire coat hanger and jammed it into the set to get a picture. Swanky accommodations!

The Hotel Cincinnatian was the kind of place where old men sat in the lobby, swapping war stories and tales of the sea. I felt like more of a pantywaist punk than ever. But I did get an enormous room with an odd feature. Dead center in the room was a toilet, right at the end of the bed. Which made me think that this had once been something other than a bedroom. Maybe a communal latrine? I didn't really want to know.

My first night there, after the show, I lay down on the bed and began to doze off. Suddenly, I heard a noise—sort of like running water. I looked up and saw water spilling in from under my door. So I got up and opened the door to investigate. And I found an old man standing there, *peeing on my door!*

I had to kind of quickly close it again to keep my legs from getting splashed!

I hollered at him, "Hey! What are you doin'? Get outta here! You're peeing on my door!"

The old man started to cower and make yelping noises, like a dog getting beaten. Then he said, "Sorry. But I *always* pee on this door!"

I looked down at the lower corner of the door and saw that it was all rotten and stained.

It was his door, all right.

He said, a little proudly, "I've been peeing on this door for four years!"

From the look of the door, he may have been underestimating.

So I said, "Well, just don't pee on it for the next couple of days, okay? That would really be great."

■ ■ ■

A New York booking agency liked to pluck comics from the clubs and send us on upstate college gigs. You'd go out on mini-tours of the State University of New York schools like Cobleskill, Delhi, Cortland, and Binghamton. Sometimes this meant playing in various quads in the center of campuses, doing what they called "nooners"—midday shows during which you stood on steps, hollering jokes at students on their way to class, who couldn't have cared less. Basically, you felt like a raving lunatic making a soapbox harangue. But even that was preferable to what I remember as the worst college gig I ever took.

A sorority hired me to play a *study hall*! During midterms. Seventy-five dollars for three shows over three consecutive

Chess, anyone?

nights. So I drove the eight hours up from Boston and met the sorority sisters, who led me to the appointed place: Study Hall C. On the door, they had affixed a small index card that read: COMEDIAN TONIGHT! I soon learned that this was the extent of the advance publicity.

I walked in and saw my audience: thirty-five kids hunched over their books, studying intently. They didn't exactly look starved for entertainment. They didn't even look like they were breathing! Dread started welling up inside me. But I sat down at one of the little study desks and waited for the sorority girls to introduce me. These were girls who had that shrill sort of Long Island accent that makes Fran Drescher sound like James Earl Jones. You wished only dogs could hear it. So they shattered the silence:

"Okaaaaaaaay, everybody! Toniiiiight, the Sisters of [Whatever-Stupid-Sorority-It-Was] are happy to present an exciting comedy showwww. We've got a *professional comeeeedian* for you!"

One surly guy looked up from his books and said, "Yeah, who? George Carlin?"

One girl pointed to where I was sitting and said, "No, it's that guy right over there!"

I gave a little wave and said, "Hi, everybody."

The surly kid groaned, "Hey, we're *studying*! We don't want any comedy show!"

Of course, I wanted to leave right then.

But the girls dragged me to the front of the study hall and handed me their "sound system." This consisted of a microphone plugged into a speaker on a handle. The mike cord was only a couple feet long, which meant that I had to carry the speaker around with me in order to talk. Worse yet, the speaker was then plugged into a wall socket with an eight-foot cord—so I couldn't move beyond an eight-foot radius. Basically, I was wedged into a corner! On top of that, the volume was so weak that only the people at whom I directly aimed the speaker could actually hear me. So I had to wave the speaker in front of me as I spoke. Which I reluctantly began to do.

"Hey, how're you guys doin' tonight—"

"Hey, you're a *real* professional! You suck! You stink!"

It was the same surly kid.

One polite student tried to quiet him down: "Shhhhhh, just let the guy talk!"

But he kept on heckling: "You suck! We're trying to study here!"

And he never stopped. He stepped on every word I said, which killed any possibility of getting laughs. I was supposed to do forty minutes, but was done in under a half-hour. During all that time, I was holding the speaker, which got heavier and heavier with each minute of desperation. At last, I finished and went over to the sorority girls, who were sneering at me.

I told them, "Look, this isn't working. These kids don't want to be bothered with a show."

One of the girls said, "Well, you were supposssssssed to do forty minutes! You stopped too soon!"

I said, "But no one was really listening! I don't think this can work three nights in a row. Why don't you just pay me twenty-five dollars for tonight and I'll go home."

They wanted no part of it. They just got shriller. "The agent saidddddd you would play three nights! We're going to cawwwwwll the agent and say you were very unprofessional."

"All right, all right, I'll come back tomorrow!"

I could only hope for a better crowd. Meanwhile, they put me up in a dorm room that I had to share with a Middle Eastern foreign exchange student who spoke no English. He just sat studying at his desk and said nothing. I might as well have been back in Study Hall C. This felt like I was doing jail time. Even my cellmate seemed hostile.

The next night, I returned to Study Hall C—and found the same thirty-five kids studying there! The antagonism started right where it had left off the night before. The same loudmouth guy saw me walk in and shouted, "You sucked last night! What are you doing here again?"

"Well, I'm supposed to be here for three nights."

"Three nights! Boo! You stink!"

Even the polite kid who'd tried to defend me the night before joined in: "Please! No more jokes!"

Then a girl, whom I'd noticed smiling at me the night before, was now staring down at her books with both of her hands clasped over her ears. She was *forcing* herself not to listen.

Not only was it the same audience, but I was doing the same act. (I had only one act.) At this point, my original heckler was predicting the material, calling out the punch lines—*and* the setups.

I started: "Hey, have you ever been—"

"Yeah, *I've been to McDonald's, you idiot!* Man, don't you get it? We heard this stuff last night! It wasn't good then!"

Helplessly, I looked over to the sorority girls, whose arms were rigidly folded. They whined, *"You have to do the show!"*

So I did, waving the portable speaker, bombing as horribly

as the night before. This show was even shorter than the last one.

Afterward, the girls marched up to me, shocked that I'd repeated the same material. For seventy-five dollars, they expected three completely different shows. I said that it didn't work that way. The *audience* is supposed to change—not the jokes. They didn't care: "Well, you better be good tomorrow night!"

Meanwhile, word of my miserable act had spread throughout the campus. People now shunned me wherever I went. On the third day, I was standing in line in the cafeteria and heard students giggling behind me: "*Look, there's that asshole who thinks he's a comedian!*" This had become a nightmare of hellish proportion. I wanted out! At least it was almost over.

That night, I went back to Study Hall C for my final performance. *And the same thirty-five kids were there!* This was like a *Twilight Zone* episode. The minute I walked in, the derision started. Only this time, *everyone in the room* had turned on me. It was like a chorus of hate: "Why don't you just get out of here! Okaaay? You *suck!*" By now, they thought I was going to be there for the rest of their lives.

So I repeated the act one more time, lugging the speaker around. It took all of fifteen minutes. Same stuff, no laughs, kids screaming out the punch lines, nightmare nightmare nightmare.

"*It's not funny, man! Don't you get it? YOU SUCK!*"

When it was over, whatever was left of me slunk toward the girls who hired me. I wanted my money and my freedom.

One of them poked me with her finger and snapped, "Look, I know it was supposed to be seventy-five dollahs. But we're only paying you *twenty-five* becawwwwse you did the same stuff three nights in a row! We think you're *verrrrry unprofessional!*"

■ ■ ■

In New York, I hooked up with one booking agent who taught me some valuable lessons about show business. Unfortunately, these were the sort of lessons that make you want to *leave* show business. He got me a lot of jobs at the predominantly Jewish resorts in the Catskill Mountains. For instance, he once had me open there for the Supremes. Of course, these weren't the *real* Supremes. For "nostalgia" gigs, which this was, you were lucky to get even one member of the original group to ever play along. And that was the case here: one original Supreme and two other girls in wigs who learned all the songs. But for the purposes of Catskills entertainment—*they were the Supremes!*

And this gave the agent another opportunity to make money. That week, he approached the nearby racetrack at Monticello and said, "Listen, I could get you the Supremes to come do a little something between races on Saturday afternoon. All it would cost is a thousand dollars!"

The racetrack people thought this was a great idea.

So the agent went back to the hotel to tell the Supremes, who were instantly offended: "No way! We're not doing that."

"Oh, no? I'll give you *five hundred dollars!*"

(The man had no conscience.)

"No, no, we don't want to do it."

"What about for seven hundred fifty?"

"Not even for a thousand, baby!"

Not to be undone, he went out and hired three black girls

who looked nothing like the Supremes—much less like the "new" Supremes—and told them to dress up. Then he put them in the backseat of a convertible and, while some greatest hits played over loudspeakers, he drove around the track at eighty miles per hour. So fast that nobody could have hoped to recognize the girls waving from the backseat!

Meanwhile, over the public-address system, an announcer kept repeating: "The Supremes! Ladies and gentlemen! The Supremes!" They circled the track a couple of times, then sped out the exit, earning this sleazy agent his grand. Those girls probably got fifty bucks apiece for their trouble.

Another time, he got me a job at a Hasidic resort—although I didn't know that until I got there. I remember driving up to the place and seeing a trailer marquee on the lawn. The sign read: TONIGHT: JAY LENO, JEWISH STORYTELLER!

What on earth had the agent told these people!

I immediately went to find the entertainment director to explain that there must have been some mix-up. I told him, "I'm not even Jewish!"

He was very nice. He said, "Oh, it doesn't really matter. Just tell good jokes."

So I went onstage and told the crowd that my agent had made a mistake, that I didn't know any Jewish stories. But they very kindly urged me to go ahead with my act anyway. Which I did. To a sort of stunned silence. If anything, they were just a little disappointed that I was telling my jokes in English.

Then there was a weeklong gig for which I was to be paid one hundred twenty dollars. This seemed like kind of a low fig-ure for a week's work, but I was just starting out and certainly wasn't a name act. Anyway, at the end of the week, during which I had done very well, the resort manager came over to me and said, "I just wanted you to know that we really enjoyed you. At first, we didn't want to spring for your twelve-hundred-dollar fee, but you were worth it!"

Twelve hundred dollars? I was getting one hundred twenty bucks—*ten percent* of the agent's take! It was supposed to be the other way around! That was the last time I worked for that agent. Although I couldn't help but be pleased that someone actually thought that I was worth twelve hundred dollars.

■ ■ ■

After a while, I began to develop an instinct for how to read an audience, good and bad. Certain rooms on certain nights had different personalities. I remember a night at Catch a Rising Star when a mobster was sitting down front with a cluster of his friends, all of them kind of ominous looking. One comic was performing, and he must have said something the mob guy didn't like, because the mobster suddenly stood up and, BOOM, he decked the comic. For obvious reasons, nobody said anything to the mob guy. Anything might set off somebody like that. And who knew whether he was packing heat? So another comic came on, business as usual, and then another—who happened to be my friend Richard Belzer.

Belzer, of course, has never been one to back away from confrontation. So he began his set by announcing, "I see we've got a *hit man* in the front row! You like to hit people? What are you, pal? *Mafia?*"

Naturally, the guy stood up again and pounded Belzer in the face. And Belzer went down. Hard. Some other comics dragged him offstage. And again nobody said anything to the tough guy, for fear of gunplay and meat hooks.

But now it was my turn. And I wasn't going to take any chances. In fact, if anything, I thought that I would err on the side of *extreme respect* for the guy.

So I came out and smiled at him. And I began by saying, "Hello, SIR! How are *you* tonight? Very nice to have you!"

He seemed to like this. I must have sounded like his favorite maitre d'. Then I just launched into my act, did fine, and got off. Sighing with relief, I walked to the back of the room. That's when I saw one of the mobster's pals slowly head toward me. Uh-oh. But he was smiling. He came up and reached into his coat. Uh-oh. Then he pulled out a one-hundred-dollar bill and said, "I enjoyed your act very much." And he stuffed the C-note into my shirt pocket.

I took it out right away and said, "Oh, thank you very much, sir." Suddenly, I felt pretty confident. So I handed it back to him and said, "But why don't you maybe give this to the church or someone who needs help?"

The guy gave me another little smile.

"You know," he said, "you're a *very* smart kid. That was a very smart thing to do. You should *never* take money from people like me."

Then he left. And I never had any problem. In fact, I just kept waiting for some comics I didn't care for to turn up missing.

■ ■ ■

There was one genuinely rough place in Boston where comics played. It was the kind of club where you were never quite sure who owned it. Moreover, you didn't *want* to know. They had a big moose of a doorman there known as Billy the Bouncer. He had slick, well-coifed hair and wore a lot of gold chains. Just a fearsome guy with a very short fuse.

One night, when I was onstage, a loud guy came into the room and was seated behind a pole. So he hollered, *"Hey, I can't see!"*

Billy the Bouncer went over to him and said, "Shut up and watch the show."

"I can't see!"

That was all it took to get Billy's goat. He said, "Oh, a troublemaker!" He grabbed the guy and threw him down the entrance stairs. Meanwhile, I was watching all this from the stage, plowing ahead with my material.

Suddenly, the guy rushed back up the stairs and bleated, "He can't throw me down the stairs!"

So Billy took a knife and stabbed the guy in the leg. Now he started screaming in agony!

Billy said, "Hey, nutcake, quit screamin'!"

I finally had to say, "Hey, what's going on back there?"

Billy, of course, couldn't bear that my set had been interrupted. Even though he had caused it. So he grabbed the guy and dragged him into the street, where he threw him into a taxi and gave the cabbie twenty bucks to get rid of him.

And that was a typical night in the life of Billy the Bouncer.

Several years later, after I had moved to California, I got a call from one of the wiseguys who managed the club. He said, "Yo, Jay! Listen, I see you're doin' pretty good out there! We're havin' a little benefit for Billy and we thought maybe you could come back and do a show to help him out."

I said, "You mean Billy the Bouncer?"

"Yeah, yeah."

"What happened?"

"Well, I guess he killed a guy and the cops are *hasslin'* him."

"*Hassling him?* Why don't you do a benefit for the guy he killed?"

The wiseguy howled: "*Hahahahahahahahahaha!* What a comedian! You're a funny guy! *Doin' a benefit for a guy that got killed!* Hey, Jay, quit kiddin' around, will ya? So, you wanna help us out?"

I said, "*Did* he kill a guy?"

"Oh, I don't know. You know cops."

I said, "Well, I'm on TV now and if I come back, it'll look kind of bad. I can't be doing benefits for somebody who killed a guy."

"Oh, you can't do it? Oh, man. Billy would really appreciate it!"

"Well, it's murder!"

"Oh, murder. All right, Mr. Big Shot!"

■ ■ ■

Slowly I started getting some press in little Boston newspapers. Media tend to attract other media, and, soon after, I was booked to be a guest on a local WBZ-TV morning public affairs–type show called *What's New*—which was a thrill for a college student, and a great way to impress girls. So, on the scheduled day, I went down to the station and waited for the producer in the lobby. After a few minutes, a really attractive girl walked in and smiled at me. At that moment, the producer came out and said, "Mr. Leno, you'll be on in about twenty minutes." This was perfect timing! The girl's eyes lit up.

To belabor the point, I said to the producer, *"Oh, I'll be going on in twenty minutes? Oh, thank you!"*

Now the girl was hooked! She asked me, "So, what are you doing?"

I swaggered a little and said, "I'm a comedian and I'm just going on TV to talk about show business." (As though this happened every day!)

"Oh, really? You're a comedian? That's fascinating!"

She told me her name and asked me questions, seeming more and more intrigued with me. This was working out great! At least she knew I wasn't a delivery boy. I figured that this could go somewhere.

And then she said, "Hey, are you doing anything Friday night?"

"Well, no."

She said, "Would you like to come to my place? I'm having just a few people over."

"Sure!"

Show business was getting better by the minute. Just as the producer came back to get me, the girl handed me her phone number.

"Oh, thanks. Gotta go—I'm on TV!"

This was going like clockwork. That night I called her and we talked some more. She told me to come over at nine Friday and sounded very excited.

Friday night, I got to her condo on time and heard lots of voices from inside the door. I walked in and the girl clapped her hands together.

She screamed, *"Everyone! Everyone! The COMEDIAN is here!"*

I looked around the room at a dozen or so people—all of whom must have been there since seven-thirty! Then it hit me: I had been booked as the entertainment for this girl's dinner party! Now her guests all sat down cross-legged on the living room floor, anticipating my show. They were whispering things like: "Is this guy funny? What show was he on?"

I turned to the girl and said, "Um, how you doin'?"

"Oh, great, great. Do you want a drink before you start?"

"Well, uh, I . . ."

Without even looking at me, she then turned to her friends and said, "Okay, everybody, this is Jay! I met him the other day and he's a comedian. Okay, Jay, go ahead!"

Suddenly, I felt like such a dope. This girl had no interest in me other than as a performer—and, moreover, she had invited me over to work for free. But I did about eight minutes, anyway. Then I bolted out of there, looking forward to impressing other girls with my exciting show business career.

■　■　■

After I'd been working the New York clubs for a while, an agent called me with the news that the TV show *A.M. Buffalo* wanted to have me on as a guest one morning. He said, "The producers saw you somewhere the other night and thought you were great! They're huge fans of yours!" Of course, this couldn't have been more flattering. To be singled out in a club! TV producers who were *fans* of mine! Naturally, I was very eager to get any kind of TV exposure—even if it meant driving eight hours up to Buffalo. Which I happily did.

When I got to the studio, an assistant led me to the green-room, where I would wait to go on. I was wearing kind of a flashy white suit, trying to make a distinctive impression. As it turned out, I couldn't have been more distinct from the other guests that day. The only other people in the greenroom that morning were seven members of an *authentic African Pygmy dance troupe*!

I sat down on a couch across from the Pygmy dancers—seven black men, none of whom was more than four feet tall. They were dressed in ceremonial skirts, and each held an enormous spear. Clearly, they were the real thing! We kind of politely nodded at one another and quietly waited to be called to the set.

As I waited, I reminded myself of how pleased I was that the A.M. *Buffalo* producers had claimed to be such big fans of mine. Maybe I was making headway in the business, after all.

At which point, a woman holding a clipboard opened the door and carefully stared around the room at the seven little dancers and me. She had a puzzled look on her face and pensively tapped a finger to her chin.

Finally, she said, "Um, I'm looking for a Mr. Leno . . . The comedian? Now which one of you would be Mr. Leno?"

There were only eight of us in the room. And only one of us wasn't holding a spear.

I said, "Uh, I'm Mr. Leno."

"Oh, *you're* Mr. Leno! Fine. Come with me."

It occurred to me then that I would probably have to work a bit harder at making myself look distinctive.

9

HOW DO YOU REMEMBER ALL THAT STUFF?

There's an old joke about comedians that I heard very early on. Basically, it tells you everything you need to understand about how a comic's mind works. I thought this would be as good a place as any to share it:

So there's this comic who's working a Las Vegas hotel for the first time. Opening night, he does his shows and just kills—blows the audiences away! Afterward, he goes back to his hotel room. He's so excited from the shows, he can't fall asleep. At three-thirty in the morning, he's still wound up. Then the phone rings. On the other end, there's a very sexy female voice: "Hi, is this Joe Blow, the comedian?"

"Yes, it is."

The sexy voice goes on: "My name is Felicity. I'm the lead dancer across the street at the Folies Bergère show. I just wanted to say that I saw your performance tonight and I thought you were really funny and sexy and cute! You really made me laugh.

*Anyway, I thought that maybe I could come up to your room and,
you know, visit with you. I'd leave in the morning, so nobody
would even know I was there."*

The comic pauses for a few seconds.

*Then he says, "Let me ask you something: Did you see the
first show or the second show?"*

Stupid, I know. But this should demonstrate how single-
minded comics are about their careers. On the other hand, we
can't live on jokes alone.

Pretty close. But not entirely.

Not that anything ever went all that smoothly for me—as
the next two stories will illustrate.

■ ■ ■

There was a girl who came into Catch a Rising Star a couple of
nights in a row. She would wander over to me, and I guess we
flirted back and forth. Eventually, she invited me back to her
midtown apartment, which was a beautiful white penthouse with
wraparound windows. The odd part was that there were no blinds
on any of the windows, nor was there a stick of furniture in the
place—just a futon on the floor and, in the middle of the living
room, six enormous banana crates plastered with Chiquita labels.

I pointed to the crates and asked her, "What are these?"

She went, "Well, they're my boyfriend's."

I said, "*Boyfriend!* Oh, man, I don't want to get involved, if
you're seeing somebody . . ."

She said, "No, no, we're breaking up. He's just letting me
stay here. He's out of the country. We're not seeing each other
anymore."

She seemed sincere enough, so I asked again, "What's in those crates?"

She said, "Well, he's in the import business. He imports bananas. He said sometimes they get overstocked and they just send them here."

I said, "Oh, I see . . ."

I ended up spending the night with her. The next morning, the sun streamed in at the crack of dawn. Blinking back the bright light, I got up to look for something to eat. There was nothing in the refrigerator or the cupboards. I looked over at the Chiquita crates and said, "Hey, let's have some bananas."

She said, "No, we better not take any."

I said, "But no one's going to miss two bananas from six huge crates!"

So I pried open one box and reached in, but couldn't feel any bananas. Then I saw that my hands were covered with grease! I looked in and saw a bunch of . . . *guns!* They were all automatic assault rifles with huge cartridges.

I said, "What's this! These aren't bananas—*these are guns!*"

I'll never forget what she said next:

"Well, maybe there's some bananas in the other crates."

I said, "*There aren't bananas in any of these!!!* What did you say your boyfriend does?"

"Well, he's in the import business."

I said, "Where's he from?"

"I think he's from Cuba. Or one of those places."

"Cuba? He's importing guns! He's a gunrunner!"

"I don't think so."

"*Get outta here! The FBI's probably watching us right now!*"

I expected to see a flash of government gunfire from the roof across the way! I got the hell out of there. Thank you, goodbye.

■　■　■

I began to see a trend in dangerous women who hung around the comedy clubs. And it wasn't limited to the New York clubs, either. I had an upcoming gig in Philadelphia, which I mentioned to my friend Mike Preminger, a comedian with whom I sometimes stayed in New York. Mike had done a *Tonight Show* and would later go on to write movies. He knew that money was always tight—especially when it came to spending nights on the road. So he said, "My brother lives in Philly—do you want to stay with him? He's got a town house."

Naturally, I thought this was a great idea. Off I went to Philadelphia, where I met Mike's brother, Daniel, a very nice guy who worked there as a lawyer. He showed me around his town house and said, "Jay, feel free to take my bedroom tonight. I'll sleep in my office in the next room." I protested, but he insisted: "No, please take my room, it's cool."

I headed off to the club and did my set. Afterward, I met this girl and we hit it off pretty well. She asked me what I was doing later. I told her that I was staying with a friend, but maybe she could come over.

So I brought her back to the town house, where we sat down in the living room. Daniel came in, assessed the situation, and slyly gave me the international go-for-it signal. Then he went off to sleep. So I took the girl upstairs to his room.

We started fooling around, but nothing much was happening. She didn't seem particularly interested at all. I said, "Is there anything wrong?"

She replied in a blasé manner, "Um, no, nothing's wrong."

I started to do a few other things, getting no real response to any of them.

"You're sure everything's okay?"

Again, ho-hum as ever: "Oh, yes, fine."

Like most guys of my generation, I was familiar with the idea of open sexual communication, as learned by reading *Penthouse* letters. In fact, I had done a bit onstage earlier that night about *Penthouse* letters. This girl had seen my act, so I figured I'd better live up to my apparent liberal-mindedness.

So I said, "Obviously, this isn't working. Is there something that you want me to do? Because I'll do that! We don't know each other, so you should just tell me what you like. Really, I don't mind at all. . . ."

And she said, "Well, um, I want you to tie me up. That's really the only way it works for me."

I futilely looked around the room for something to tie her with. Then I opened the closet and saw a rack of neckties. So I grabbed a few and did what she wanted me to do. Which was to tie her hands behind her back. Amazingly, this worked. Not only was she responding, she was screaming at the top of her lungs! She was just going nuts. I felt like a guy in a *Penthouse* letter, like one of the world's greatest lovers—basically, like somebody else!

All of a sudden, Daniel was pounding on the door. "Jay! Jay! Let me in! Is everything okay?"

She rolled off the bed onto the floor as I went over to the door and opened it a crack. I whispered, "Everything's fine. She just got a little . . . um, excited. But I feel terrible that I woke you up!" He gave me a big grin and, once again, the international go-for-it signal: "Nah, it's cool. Just try to keep it down, okay?" I crept back to where I'd left off—this time, to the floor, where she was writhing around. This nonsense went on—more quietly—for a little while longer. Finally, I said, "Let me untie you now."

She said, "No, don't untie me. Leave me tied up here on the floor all night. I like it here."

Strange request, but at least I'd now have the whole bed to myself. So I drifted off to sleep. The next thing I knew, it was nearly seven in the morning and I heard another knock at the door. When I opened my eyes, I saw Daniel peek in. He was wearing a white shirt and suit, but no tie. Because I was the only one in bed, he assumed that the girl had gone home. So he walked in, whispering to me, "Sorry, I've gotta go to court early today. I forgot to get my blue tie."

At which point, he found himself tripping over the girl on the floor. Worse yet, he saw his blue tie wrapped around her wrist! She brightly smiled at him and said, "*Hi!*" She was now even more thrilled that a new element of oddity had entered the equation.

Daniel looked at me like I was an axe murderer: "*What are you doing?*"

"Well, um, she wanted me to tie her up . . ."

"*With my blue tie?*"

Completely flustered, he turned and quickly left the room. I started to tug the tie loose to give it to him. The girl said, "Oh, please, don't untie me!"

I said, "*Will you just cut it out!*"

I got the tie and chased after him—but it was too horribly wrinkled and mangled to wear. And he just tore off, open-collared, to court. Of course, I felt awful.

But he was very decent about it when he got home. He just said, "Jay, it's probably best that you don't bring anybody back here later."

■ ■ ■

It's true that a certain kind of woman tends to fall for comedians. Comedians, meanwhile, tend to fall for every woman who ever laughed at their jokes. Especially for any woman who ever asked, "How do you remember all that stuff?" Bingo! That was it! (This is such a well-understood code phrase among comedians that it's almost a joke. For instance, whenever I see Jerry Seinfeld do his act, I always ask him afterward, "Hey! How do you remember all that stuff?") I've known guys who spend virtually all their free time offstage trying to get laid. Both Freddie Prinze and Andy Kaufman were like that. And they made no secret of it. Other comics tried to be far more covert in their rampant womanizing. Although their covers would inevitably be blown. Sometimes by well-meaning colleagues.

When I first moved to Los Angeles, comedians would often gather at Canter's Delicatessen on Fairfax. I remember hanging out there one day with my friend Jimmy Brogan, when a girl came over to ask if we knew where one particular comedian was. The guy she mentioned was one of the world-class Lotharios, who also happened to be married with children. He was just a notorious dog. But, for some reason, it didn't occur to Brogan and me that this girl might be one of his extracurricular activities. Just hearing his name made us crack up.

I said, "Oh, *that* guy! Maybe he's with his *kids* today!"

Jimmy said, "I'm sure his *wife* doesn't even know where he is . . ."

And we laughed some more.

The girl said, "He's *married?*"

I said, "Yeah, but he still screws everything that moves!"

Now the girl's lower lip started quivering. Tears welled up in her eyes.

And she said, "But he's my *boyfriend!*"

She was now sobbing uncontrollably!

Uh-oh. What idiots we were! Instantly, I tried to cover.

"Oh, we're just kidding! You fell for the old he's-married-and-screws-everything-that-moves trick! Ha ha ha!"

This didn't seem to work very well. She ran out the door, bawling her eyes out. The comic probably never knew what hit him. And he certainly didn't know who triggered that blowup! I hope.

■ ■ ■

I was always amazed at the number of comics who would disregard some basic rules of comedy. Some of these rules are unspoken, but very obvious. I coined a term for one of them, which is my Thirty-nine-and-a-half Rule. The gist of this one is that standup comedians can get away with talking about having sex and about admiring breasts and asses for only so long. If you're twenty-five, women won't be as offended. They'll say, "Oh, he said *ass!* Isn't he cute!"

But when you're older, say, thirty-nine-and-a-half, you can't do it anymore. Your hair is thinning and you've put on extra pounds and *no one* wants to hear about your sexual proclivities. The same girls who laugh at younger guys going on about sex will wince and say, "Ugh, that old jerk is so gross!"

I've seen so many guys lose track of their sense of time

and place. And then they'll make the most ridiculously anti-quated references. When I was making my rounds of New York clubs, there was an older guy who would come to The Improv and die miserably onstage. He was in his mid-fifties, wore black sharkskin suits, and had made a small name for himself working joints along the Jersey shore. But, at The Improv, he stood out glaringly from all of us younger guys by telling jokes like, "I just bought one of those new foreign jobs with the four-on-the-floor and bucket seats—and when you hit ninety, the radio plays 'Nearer My God to Thee'!" Truly horrible stuff.

Still, he was a very nice guy. I felt kind of sorry for him. One night, he started a joke this way: "Hey, fellas, ever notice when you go to a bar those *guys in uniform with the medals*! Boy, they get *all the gals*, don't they?"

Never mind that this was the early seventies.

The audience screamed, "Boooo! Get off the stage, you warmonger! Stop your war machine!"

Afterward, he came over to me and asked, quite genuinely, "Why are they booing at me? I don't get it."

I said, "Well, you know, it's really not popular to talk about men in uniform anymore. For whatever reason, after Vietnam and Kent State, people aren't really into the military. Maybe you need to change your reference to something more contemporary . . ."

His eyes lit up: "Oh, yeah! That's good! That's good! I'll just update it."

A couple of weeks later, he came back and took me aside. He said, "Jay, watch my act tonight! I made some changes."

Then he went onstage and began: "Hey, fellas, do you ever

notice when you go into a bar . . . those *Green Berets*! Whew! They get *all the girls*, don't they?"

The audience booed even louder: "Get off, warmonger!"

He looked over to me, baffled. Later, I told him, "I think you've got to update just a little more."

■ ■ ■

I found that other comedians recommended me for jobs as much as any agent or manager did. Robert Klein was always very nice to me that way. And Gabe Kaplan brought me onto the *Mike Douglas Show* in Philadelphia one week when he was guest co-host. Just before that, I'd done my only other national television appearance at the Bitter End in New York, as part of the summer series *Dean Martin's Comedy World*. This was maybe the most absurd TV shot in the history of standup. It was for me, at least.

The conceit of the show was that host Jackie Cooper would sit at a bank of video monitors, where he would tune in to exciting comedy acts happening in all corners of the nation. He'd say, "Now let's plug in to see what some of the bright young comedians are doing!" Then he'd cut to the Bitter End, where *Get Smart's* Barbara Feldon presided over a handful of comics who took turns doing their acts onstage. I was one of the comics. And, of course, I was thrilled to be a part of this parade.

But there were some odd factors involved. First of all, there was no audience. To create a more intimate feeling, however, it was decided that separate reaction shots would be taped of Barbara Feldon sitting with all the young comics. We'd be seen laughing politely at our peers onstage. And, of course, a general laugh track would be added later. Dean Martin's longtime executive producer, Greg Garrison, was the director. And, one by one, he sent the comics up to do their acts. My turn came, I told my jokes, then left the stage.

Greg said, "Okay, very funny, very good. Take a break, Jay!"

A couple more comics did their shots. Then he said, "I'm going to leave now. The second assistant director will shoot the second part of the show."

The second A.D., however, couldn't quite tell one of us from another. He announced, "Okay, let's get everybody together to do the reaction shots."

We all went over to the seats by Barbara Feldon, who would tell viewers the name of each comic before we'd be seen onstage. The A.D. told me to sit right next to Barbara, which I thought was terrific. Then it was time to shoot us laughing at the acts.

He said, "All right, everybody, give a big laugh!"

So we did: "HA HA HA HA HA!"

"All right, now a little laugh."

"Ha ha ha ha!"

"Give me a titter."

"Ho ho ho."

We went through every imaginable kind of laugh, which would be intercut with the comedy. Then it was time for Barbara to read our introductions off the cue cards.

So Barbara said, "We're here at the Bitter End in New York, and right now we're watching a very funny young man named Jay Leno! Let's take a look!"

The only problem was that, in the shot of Barbara saying

this, you could clearly see me sitting next to her. How could she be watching me onstage while I was three inches from her elbow? Moreover, how could *I* be watching myself onstage? She obviously didn't know me, so I tapped her on the shoulder.

"Um, I'm Jay Leno—"

"CUT!" the A.D. screamed. "Please don't talk to Miss Feldon during the intros!"

"Okay."

I was frightened to say anything else. Barbara started the intro all over again: ". . . we're watching a very funny young man named Jay Leno!"

When the show was edited together for the air, there I was beside her watching my own performance. Worse yet, every time they cut to her laughing at me—*I was right there laughing at myself!* People thought I was doing some Fellini bit. No one seemed to figure out how ridiculous this looked.

Anyway, the show was supposed to air at ten o'clock on the night of August 8, 1974. Which it did. And, at the precise moment Barbara Feldon said, ". . . very funny young man named Jay Leno . . . ," NBC News broke in with a special bulletin.

"We have learned that President Nixon will resign from office tomorrow . . ."

And the rest of the show was preempted entirely. Although it did air again several weeks later, bad reaction shots and all. But I was always proud to be obliterated by that news bulletin.

The way it turned out, this officially made me the last guy screwed by Nixon before he left office.

10

THE FACE IN THE TRASH CAN

In the seventies, the moment came for every comic: You had to risk it all and go west. A New York career could take you only so far. I watched a number of my peers from The Improv make the big decision to try their luck in California. Some were better than me and some were worse. But we were all pretty much in the same class. On any given night, any one of us could have done better than the others. Some of them just got that burning-in-the-gut feeling and knew that it was their time to seek fortune. One guy I knew had just left New York for California and, within a few months, POW!, he was booked on *The Tonight Show*—the pinnacle of show business for any comedian!

That night, I was back in my Boston apartment, watching the show. The comic did okay, nothing special, but there he was—performing ten feet away from Johnny Carson's desk! I thought, "Geez, I often did much better than this guy when we played clubs together." And I couldn't shake the thought. Now my gut was burning and I knew it.

I've always said that the worst thing you can do in show business is make thirty thousand dollars a year by doing something else to support yourself. I'd already quit my job at Foreign Motors to focus on comedy. Now it was time to make the next big decision. If I stayed in Boston, I would want to have a nicer apartment or a better car—and suddenly I'd be stuck there, married to these possessions. In such pivotal life moments, you either stay or you go. So I simply imagined that there'd been a fire in my apartment—which wasn't far from the reality of what a dump it had become! What would I have really lost? A warped, steam-buckled kitchen? A psychotic screaming refrigerator? A bedroom wall ventilated by Freddie Prinze's bullets? A brown, dead, year-round Christmas tree?

Sometime before *The Tonight Show* ended that night, I just said, "That's it. Let me call the airlines and book the next flight to California."

Which is what I did. I told the neighbors that they could take anything of mine that they wanted. I packed up whatever else I needed and just walked out the door. And that was that. I went west.

■ ■ ■

Then I landed at Los Angeles International Airport. And I realized that I had no place to stay. (Spontaneity can at times be overrated.) I hopped in a cab and told the driver the only destination I could think of: "Take me to the Sunset Strip!" I figured that this would be the Los Angeles equivalent of Times Square or Boston's Kenmore Square—the one area where everything happened. We pulled out of LAX and I drank in my first impression of Los Angeles—a strip joint with a huge sign that screamed: NUDES! FROM SEVEN A.M. I imagined guys going in there at seven in the morning and seeing a naked woman onstage, her hair in curlers, cooking eggs. I thought, "Well, I'm not in Andover anymore!"

Fifty dollars later(!), the cab dropped me off at Vermont and Sunset. This was technically still the Sunset Strip—but roughly ten miles east of where I wanted to go. Where I wanted to go was The Comedy Store in West Hollywood. And somehow I managed to get there. Then I remembered that my friend Billy Braver, another comic, lived in an apartment complex right across the street. I lugged my bags over there, and he let me in and said I could crash on his couch.

The first thing I did was go look out of his enormous plate-glass window. I wanted to glimpse Hollywood in all its glory. The window faced across a courtyard and pool toward the corresponding apartments directly on the other side of the complex. And there, staring back from the window of the opposite apartment, was Joe E. Ross, the legendary simianlike Officer Toody of *Car 54, Where Are You?* He was completely naked!

Now, this was not a guy you'd ever want to *picture* naked—much less see for yourself. And I thought, "So this is Hollywood! Glamour capital of the world! What's wrong with this picture?"

After that initial shock of introduction, Joe E. Ross was the first Hollywood star to become my friend. A former vaudeville player, he loved all the young comics, loved to tell old stories, and, most of all, loved prostitutes. So it only followed that his greatest joy was to regale us with tales of hookers he had known. Tales of times he couldn't get it up and how various hired women helped him solve the problem. I'd cover my ears and holler, "Joe, I'm not interested in the details! *Please!*"

He died not long after I met him, but his funeral was one of the great experiences of my life. Every veteran hooker in town showed up at Forest Lawn. These were women in their fifties who wore fishnet stockings and leopard-skin bustiers. According to tradition, the rabbi presiding over the service asked whether any of the mourners wished to say a few words about Joe. And, of course, most of the prostitutes wanted to share their memories.

The first one got up and said, "Joey always paid! Always paid! Other guys—you'd blow 'em and they'd stiff you. Joey, even if he couldn't get it up, he always gave you the money! Class all the way!"

The rabbi, of course, shuddered, realizing what a huge mistake he'd made in opening the floor for these touching testimonials. But it just got better.

The next woman stepped forward and began a story about how she was once performing oral sex on Joe while he was driving. Somehow her head got caught in the steering wheel and wedged against the horn ring. The horn started blaring—*beeeeeep beeeeeep beeeeeep*—as she struggled to get loose. Then a cop pulled them over and, while her head was still stuck in Joe's lap, screamed at Joe. Which sort of brought new meaning to a moving violation.

Apparently, Joe E. had once married a woman with one glass eye, and she was also there that day. She clearly still cared for him deeply, because she cried the whole time. And this made for a wonderfully odd spectacle: Tears seemed to stream only from her good eye, which she covered with one hand. But she left the glass eye exposed, just blankly staring out at everyone present, never blinking. Later, as we all wandered up past the casket, she would extend her free hand in greeting, still sobbing into the other hand. While she shook our hands, the glass eye just stared eerily at us. Very peculiar situation, but Joe E. would have loved it.

■ ■ ■

The first Los Angeles joke I came up with summed up my earliest sentiments about life westward:

"I've always lived on the East Coast. I can't get used to California. Out here, the beach is on the wrong side."

Stupid, but sort of true: There were things that took some getting used to, things that made no sense to me. During my first week, I walked around Hollywood a lot. One day, I passed a house on Gower where a yard sale was going on. I realized that the man who was unloading his old possessions was the famous comedy magician Carl Ballantine! I thought to myself, "This guy's on TV—and he's selling his stuff! How am I going to last in this town? This is just hopeless!" (I would soon learn that these yard sales are an everyday phenomenon in L.A. Everybody, except me, loves to get rid of their old junk.)

From the start, I was homeless in Los Angeles, relying on the kindness of other comics. Among them was Freddie Prinze, who let me sleep on his couch for a couple of nights. (Thankfully, I got out without any further incident of gunplay.) Or I'd work over at The Comedy Store, then often sleep on the back steps afterward. Sometimes I'd go down to Hollywood Boulevard and wander at night. More than once, police cars stopped and the cops called me over, mistaking me for a drug dealer. I'd get in the backseat of the squad car and explain that I was a comedian.

"So you're a comedian? Tell us some jokes!"

Even cops held show business auditions in Hollywood!

So I'd do parts of my act in the backseat throughout the rest of their shift. This was a bit of an inconvenience—but, hey, an audience was an audience! At least I never got run in for bad material.

Before that could happen, my New York manager at the time, Murray Becker, was able to find me a little house in which to live. The place was in Hollywood, near the foot of the Hills, and belonged to Becker's boss, Jerry Purcell. I was told that the previous owner had been the actress Karen Black. (As per Hollywood custom, houses don't become known as anyone's until they move out.) I stayed there rent-free with another Purcell client, Chick Raines, a singer-songwriter who later found great success in Nashville. Chick and I, of course, were a classic version of the Odd Couple—the country-western musician and the hopeful comic. Of the pair, I was obviously the Oscar Madison–slob guy. We lasted together for about half a year. Chick finally threw me out the day he saw me washing dishes with the same sponge I had used to clean the toilet. This seemed perfectly normal to me. A sponge is a sponge! But he couldn't take any more and hollered, *"That's it! Get out!"*

Still another strange new California custom to compre-hend . . .

■   ■   ■

An agent said, "If you wanna work on shows like Happy Days, you gotta look more like Potsie."

Before I got a car in L.A., I would hitchhike my way around town. Somebody told me that there were casting agents over in the Century City office towers. So I went out to Santa Monica Boulevard in West Hollywood—a neighborhood notorious in ways I was yet to understand—and tried to hitch a ride in that direction. My thumb wasn't out for three minutes when a car screeched up next to me. A very friendly guy opened his passenger door and said, "Where you goin'? Wanna go around the world?"

"What?" I asked, getting in.

"Do you want to go around the world?"

Odd question. I said, "No. Just to Century City."

"Well, how about a trip around the world?"

He seemed to be winking at me.

I said, "What are you talking about?"

"*You* know!"

Figuring that the man was completely nuts, I quickly decided that I'd better get out. So I said, "Oh! I forgot something at home! Thanks, anyway!"

He pulled off and I started hitchhiking again. I'd gotten about a block away when another car stopped. The driver smiled and said, "Hi, how're you doing?" Another friendly guy! I got in and he repeated, "So how are ya?" This time he gave me a couple of taps on the thigh.

I said, "Uh, I'm fine."

He said, "Good to see you! Where are you from?"

He tapped my thigh again. A little more vigorously.

"Boston."

"Oh, Boston! I've been there. Do you know a club there called the Hole?"

"No, never heard of that."

"What about a place called the Ram Rod?"

"Ram Rod? No, I never heard of that, either. Where is it?"

"Oh, back of Boylston, near the docks."

He went for my thigh again.

"Hey, hey, hey! Cut that out, will you? I'll get out *here*, thanks!"

I threw the door open fast, piled out, and extended my thumb again. Four minutes later, another car pulled up next to me. Either people were extremely friendly here or I was just attracting weirdos. This guy started with the same familiar line: "Hey, how're you doing? Where do you wanna go?"

"Well, Century City."

"Anyplace special there?"

"No, I just heard there were show business casting agents . . ."

"Oh, you're trying to get into show business, huh? Film work?"

"Sure, anything I can get."

I realized that he was looking me over closely.

Then he said, "I like guys like you."

I wasn't sure what he meant, but said, "Oh, thank you very much."

He pointed out the window and said, "Guys like *that* are way too obvious." We were driving past a man who was all but naked, wearing a little thong pouch and a feather in his hair. "See what I mean? Too obvious for me!"

I said, "What's too obvious?"

Then, like a thunderbolt, it finally dawned on me: "This guy thinks I'm a male prostitute! No wonder everybody was picking me up! Get me outta here!"

I told him, "This is close enough! I'll get out *here!*"

I bought a car the next day.

■ ■ ■

I had no pretensions to becoming an actor, but other comics told me that I'd probably make a good character in commercials, TV shows, movies, and whatnot. I think that they meant this in the nicest possible way. I think. Anyway, if you were hired, the payday was great. Occasionally, I got lucky and did some stuff on sitcoms. Jimmie "J.J." Walker got me a quick role on *Good Times*, in which I played a guy in a V.D. clinic. I wasn't sure how to explain this to my mom—but, hey, *the payday was great!*

Usually, I was typecast as kind of a dumb and benign street-guy thug, which I played on an episode of *Laverne &*

I played a goofy boyfriend in an episode of Laverne & Shirley. *Central casting had me listed under "Greaser Type."*

Shirley and also on *One Day at a Time*, as Mackenzie Phillips's biker boyfriend. I'm not sure how crazy I was about the type-casting. I remember once going out on a casting call, where I was greeted with: "We're really looking for *American*-looking people!" I told them, "Well, I was *born* here!" I was so insulted. Looking around the room, I saw dozens of blond surfer-dude types. But I'd never known what it was like to be discriminated against. I thought, "If people of color go through this every day, it must be extremely appalling."

Another time I was told to go audition for a comedy part. At this point, I had a commercial agent who sent me out on lit-erally everything—even if I was completely wrong for a role. His theory was, if you just showed up, you could talk your way into anything. So I went to the casting office and sat down in the waiting area. That's when I noticed that every other guy there was short, very thin, pale, and wore horn-rimmed glasses. I thought this was a bit odd. For hours, I waited as these little guys were called in, one by one, for their sessions with the casting director. Finally, it was my turn. I walked into the room and the director threw his hands up in disgust.

He sputtered, "Okay, that's it! What do you think you're trying to pull here?"

I was baffled by this guy's anger. I asked, "What do you mean?"

He said, "Who the hell ever told you that you looked like Woody Allen? Why are you wasting my time?"

I said, "Nobody told me I look like Woody Allen."

"This is a Woody Allen look-alike casting call, and I'm so sick of you deluded people coming in here! Do you *really* think you look like Woody Allen?"

"No, I don't look anything like Woody Allen! Nobody told me this was for look-alikes—"

"Get out! Just get outta here!"

I fled, completely embarrassed. I found this aspect of the business even more humbling than risking death onstage doing standup. At least there I was more in control of my own fate. Even my own agency demonstrated new ways to humiliate me. Not long after an ICM agent signed me, he was transferred to a different department and I was handed off to an underling. As these things worked, even if I became a success, all the credit still went to the guy who signed me. So the new guy had no reason to be all that interested in my career. But I sent him a copy of my résumé and a standard eight-by-ten glossy headshot photo, then went in to meet with him. Halfheartedly, he told me, "Well, there's not much now, but we'll keep you in mind."

I naively said, "Really? Do you think you can find something for me?"

"Oh, yeah! We have great faith in you!"

As I sat talking to him, my eyes wandered around his desk and down toward the trash can beside it. From the top of the can, I saw a torn picture of someone. What little I could see of the hair in the picture looked familiar. Out of curiosity, I leaned forward to get a better view. And then I saw . . . *my nose and my eyes!* It was my eight-by-ten, torn in half and dumped!

Naturally, I wasn't nervy enough to call the guy on it. But I prodded him a bit.

"So you really think you can find something for me?"

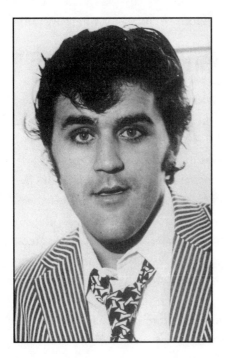

Yo! Wanna buy a used car?

"Yeah, yeah. We've got your picture and résumé on file!"

"You do have it, then?"

"Oh, yeah! You sent it over the other day, right?"

"Uh, yeah . . ."

I stood up to leave and peered down into the "circular file" at my dismembered smile. What hopelessness! To my own agent, I had been reduced to this—the Face in the Trash Can! I always thought your agent was supposed to lie *for* you, not *to* you. But I was pleased that they had great faith in me.

■ ■ ■

My face suddenly became a controversial topic. For over twenty years, it had caused me no real problems. But, in Hollywood, that seemed to change. The classic moment of reckoning came as I sat with one of my agents at a network casting meeting. For some reason, in these sessions, people don't talk *to* you—they talk *about* you. Like you're dead. And, just as though I wasn't even there, this casting guy announced, "We really like Jay, but we feel his face could be *frightening to children*."

This I'd never heard before. I had to defend myself.

I said, "I've got nieces and nephews. I play with them and they're not frightened by me."

The casting guy smiled compassionately and said, "Well, you know, they're your *family*."

"I guess you're right. I guess even the Elephant Man probably had people that cared for him, too! Thank you very much!"

Another time, I went to a casting call where a guy started off by saying, "Look, I'm gonna be honest with you . . ."

My first screen kiss was with Fran Drescher in American Hot Wax. *(For a complete description, see Fran's book, page 28.)*

Whenever they wanted to be *honest* with you, you knew something stupid was coming. Which was true at that moment. After a dramatic sigh, he said, *"You should get your jaw fixed."*

He wrote down a name and handed me the scrap of paper. "Go see this guy. He's done wonders for some of the biggest stars." He mentioned one famous name and said, "You know, he didn't always look like that!"

Really? Obviously, I knew I had the strong Leno chin. But I was used to it. Now I was getting a little insecure. So I went to this Beverly Hills doctor, who grabbed my face and turned it this way and that. As he did this, he was making little *tsk-tsk* noises.

Finally, he said, "Well, I see the problem."

Problem?

I said, "What problem? I have girlfriends who like the way I look. I've always done well in life . . ."

"Oh, but television is another world! We can fix this and make you much more handsome."

"Well, all right. What would you have to do?"

He took chalk and began to draw on my face! Then he said, "First we need to *break the jaw* here, and here, and here. Then we *rehang* it . . . using steel thread that's a tenth of a millimeter in width—"

Break and rehang it? Steel thread! Ow!

I asked, "So how long will that take?"

"Oh, no more than a week!"

"Then how long will it be before I can perform again?"

He chuckled at me like I was a moron. "Well," he said, "you won't be able to speak for about a year."

"*A year!? I can't not talk for a year!*"

"Oh, but after that, you'll have a great new look—and you'll work forever!"

"I can't take a year off! I'll forget my act!"

"Well, it's your call. You've got to think long-term career here."

I guess I'm still thinking.

▪ ▪ ▪

My frightening countenance eventually made its way onto the Big Screen, horrifying children throughout the nation. Mine would be a negligible film career, but embarrassing evidence exists nonetheless. If you don't blink, I can be spotted in the George Segal–Jane Fonda movie *Fun with Dick and Jane*. In this, my first movie role, I'm the guy distressing a hardwood floor with a chain. Then, in *Americathon*, I played a guy who fights his mother in the ring—boxing gloves and all—for money. And, yes, I decked her. Very funny script, but not a very good movie.

In *American Hot Wax*, the story of legendary rock 'n' roll deejay Alan Freed, I was his chauffeur—a likable lug with the hots for Fran Drescher, who played the secretary. The director let us improvise a lot, which helped expand my screen time with Fran. In one stupid scene, I grabbed her boobs, under the lame pretense of admiring her garments. I said, "This is wool . . . this is silk . . . and *these must be felt!*" Then she slugged me. We also had a big kissing scene. She later wrote in her book that I was the best professional kisser she ever had. Which was a nice thing to say. Unfortunately, professional kissing was never much of a career option.

I also had a pretty good part in the international-heist movie *The Silver Bears*. I played Martin Balsam's son, an

Another bad hair day, this time in Switzerland on the set of The Silver Bears.

extremely stupid thug whose father wanted him to learn the banking business. How I got the role still amazes me. One day I was sitting in front of The Comedy Store when a guy walked up to me. He said, "You have a good face for a movie. Would you like to be in a movie?"

I thought, "Uh-oh, not another one of these guys! Do I really look like a male prostitute?" At least he didn't ask me if I wanted to "go around the world."

I rolled my eyes and said, "Yeah, sure, I'll be in a movie, pal. Whatever."

He said, "We start in Switzerland in two weeks."

He did ask me to go around the world!

To get rid of him, I said, "Sure, I'll go to Switzerland. I'll be in your movie. Why not!"

"Great. Give me your phone number."

Oh boy! Here it came!

I said, "Why don't you give me *your* phone number!"

"Okay, I'll give you my number." Which he did. And I discarded it immediately. A few days later, he came back to The Comedy Store and cornered me: "You didn't call!"

"Oh, I must have lost the phone number."

"Well, you have to call the producers!" He gave me the number of a production office. Suddenly, I realized that he might be on the level. So I called the number—and found out that this guy was actually the director of the movie, Ivan Passer. Like an idiot, I'd been blowing off a real director! He'd seen my act and thought I was right for the movie. Luckily, he still wanted me. So a week later I was on a plane to Switzerland, co-starring in *The Silver Bears* with Michael Caine, Cybill Shepherd, Louis Jourdan, Martin Balsam, Tony Massia, and Tommy Smothers.

Me with Michael Caine, Tony Massia, and Louis Jourdan (without the parakeet) in The Silver Bears.

Michael Caine and I hit it off from the start. More than anything else, we enjoyed playing tricks on Louis Jourdan, the great, classy French actor. We were filming at a beautiful mansion overlooking Lake Como that was owned by an astonishingly rich man. He even had an actual Gutenberg Bible in the living room. Also in the living room was his pet parakeet, which endlessly fascinated Louis. Every day Michael and I would watch him go over to the birdcage and say, "Hal-lo, leetle parakeet! Hal-lo!" And the bird would just sit there, unmoved.

One day, Michael said, "Let's have some fun with Louis!" We went into town and bought the tiniest microcassette recorder imaginable. Then, in my best bird voice, I laid down an ongoing parakeet monologue on the tape. Over and over, I repeated, "*Bak!* Louis is an asshole! *Bak!* Louis is an asshole!

Bak! Bak!" We hid the recorder in the cage and waited for Louis to come into the room. That day, same as ever, he went over to the cage and said, "Hal-lo, leetle parakeet! Hal-lo!" And, as usual, the bird said nothing.

Louis started to walk away. When his back was turned, I reached in and switched on the machine.

Suddenly, he heard: "*Bak!* Louis is an asshole! *Bak!*"

He spun around, shocked! Then he rushed back to the cage: "Leetle bird! How could you say such a thing! Please, stop this!"

"*Bak! Bak!* Louis is an asshole!"

He was so upset that he kept asking us, "But why eez the bird saying this! I have done nothing to heeem!"

Of course, Michael and I were dying. But I had to kill time somehow when trapped in a foreign land. And, for me, idiotic jokes are part of the international language.

11

I'M FROM THE UNITED STATES. ANY UNITED STATES PEOPLE HERE?

You never know these things at the time that they happen. But, looking back, those years I spent in the mid to late seventies at The Comedy Store and The Improv were sort of a golden age. The people working in my midst in Los Angeles comprised a kind of Comedy High School. At one point or another, they were all there: The upperclassmen like Steve Martin, Robert Klein, David Steinberg, George Carlin, Richard Pryor. The sophomores like me, Andy Kaufman, Freddie Prinze, Jimmie Walker, Richard Lewis, Robin Williams, Elayne Boosler, Michael Keaton, Richard Belzer, Sandra Bernhard, George Miller, Franklyn Ajaye, Tom Dreesen, George Wallace. The up-and-coming freshmen like Jerry Seinfeld, Paul Reiser, Jimmy Brogan, Larry Miller, Carol Leifer. And so many others, all of whom will want to kill me because I forgot to mention their names. (I officially apologize now!)

Then there was the audition night at The Comedy Store when I first saw David Letterman, fresh from Indianapolis.

He drove up in his old red pickup truck and had a big reddish beard. I later liked to tease him and say that he was also wearing a rope belt and looked like Dinty Moore. Actually, there was no rope belt, but he did look like Dinty Moore. Or Paul Bunyan's son. He took the stage, obviously feeling awkward, eyes darting about, not really playing to the audience. But his material was a revelation, totally different from the sort of street attitude of most comedians. What especially stood out was his very clever phraseology. In the same way that I like to listen to John Cleese talk, I was immediately impressed with Dave, cadences and red beard and all.

After he finished, I went up to introduce myself and we kind of exchanged comedy notes. He was very nice, although somewhat quiet and shy. He usually kept to himself, but we both soon met Jimmie Walker, then starring in *Good Times*, who hired us to write material for his standup act. Once or twice a week, Dave and I would go to Jimmie's house and pitch jokes at him. Other guys who were there included Wayne Klein, who now writes for *The Tonight Show*, and my college roommate and buddy Gene Braunstein, who'd also moved west. Fourteen-year-old Byron Allen, whose mother was a friend of Walker's, would sit in because he wanted to be a comedian one day. And he threw in jokes, too. It was a lot of fun. And, of course, somebody kept notes, recording our jokes in a loose-leaf binder.

Years later, just to goof with Dave, I dug up the notebook and brought it onto his NBC *Late Night* show. I thought it would be funny to share with America some of the material he had written for Jimmie. Even Dave thought it was sort of funny. Sort of. Here, for historical purposes only, is how that nostalgic exchange went:

Me: These are the *actual* jokes we got paid a hundred bucks a week to write—

Dave: Wait a minute! You got a hundred bucks a week?

Me: Uh, maybe it was every two weeks. Anyway, these are the actual jokes that *you* wrote—

Dave: Wait a minute! Who else?

Me: Uh, I wrote them as well.

Dave: And many others.

Me: But there are some pages here that are *yours exclusively*. I thought here's a chance to perhaps use some of the—

Dave: Great, I'll look it over later!

Me: But maybe the folks would like to hear them . . . (*Audience applauds.*) Actually, some of them are not bad!

Dave: In my own defense here, not that I need to be defended—yet—but I was more the recording secretary. (*He slides his chair behind mine and looks over my shoulder as I flip through the notebook.*)

Me: You've never been this close to me before! Now, this one's not bad: "I can't believe those TV dinners!"

Dave: *Wait a minute!* Remember: These were done for Jimmie Walker.

Me: These were written by *you*, as an example of *your* work. These got you hired. (*Reading quickly.*) "I can't believe those TV dinners! You get an entire turkey dinner for eighty-five cents. It would cost more than that just to kill the turkey. Which means the turkey in your TV dinner either died or committed suicide." (*Rim shot, a little laughter.*)

Dave: You threw the joke away! You didn't sell the joke!

Me: Remember we had to write this whole TV dinner hunk for Jimmie?

Dave: But *you* never put anything down on paper! You never wrote anything down. You went to the meetings and sneered at everyone else's contributions!

Me: If you can find some of the stuff I wrote, you're *more than welcome* to read it.

Dave: What year was this?

Me: March 1, 1976. Actually, this one is really funny, but I can't read it on the air.

Dave: Let me see it. (*He slides over, reads it, chuckles.*) Try it.

Me: "In Sweden, the legal age for sexual consent is now fourteen years old. Can you believe that? Kids come home from school, have some cookies, and they say, 'Hey, Mom, I'm going to Inger's house and get laid.'" (*Rim shot, big laugh.*)

Dave: If we had a drummer in those meetings, we could have pushed a lot more of this crap.

Me: Here's a pretty good one: "Listerine is in trouble with the FCC because of their advertising—'Kills millions of germs on contact!' Who wants a mouthful of dead germs?"

Dave: This stuff is pitiful! Read some of yours, Jay! Do you have any Jay Leno jokes in there?

Me: Gee, you know, I don't know what I *did* with mine . . . I guess I must have forgotten to bring mine along! I don't know what I was thinking . . .

■   ■   ■

My first real television shot after I got to Hollywood was on *The Midnight Special,* which aired Friday nights after *The Tonight Show.* Wolfman Jack was the host, and most of the acts were rock bands, but they also used the occasional comic. The show was taped in a fairly seedy area of Gower Street. And probably because of that, they couldn't get decent audiences. So they would promise indigents and homeless people a box lunch and an apple if they would come be the audience. Plus, to give the show a more intimate feel, there were no seats. Which meant that all these people would sit on the floor and sort of mingle with the acts as they made their way to the stage.

So, after the Wolfman introduced me, I walked out to begin my set. And not two feet away from me on the floor was a disheveled-looking man eating his apple. As usual, I started out with the greeting, "Hey, how're you doin'?"

And since this man was right next to me, I reached out to shake his hand. Whereupon he just recoiled, pulled his apple away, and screamed, "Aagghhhh!"

I said, "What? What?"

And I reached out in his direction again.

"*Aaaaggghhhhhh!*"

He was shielding his apple from me!

I said, "I'm not gonna take your apple!"

But he crawled back into the crowd and started eating the apple very quickly, so that I couldn't get it from him. I thought: "Big-time TV doesn't get any classier than this! Try to get a few laughs and a guy thinks all you want is his apple."

■ ■ ■

There are technical nuances in television that took some getting used to. For instance, at one point, I found myself booked on Dinah Shore's syndicated daytime talk show. That day, I went in and met with the talent coordinator, who said, "Okay, what's your last joke, so the band knows when to play you off?" In showbiz parlance, this is called the *outcue*, which mainly serves to cover any dead air. So, as soon as a comedian ends, the band always jumps right in—*ba daaah! baaam paah! daaah dooo!* Comedians hate this because it steps on the laugh and drowns it out. Which is like a check not clearing at the bank. Very embarrassing. And, certainly, unsatisfying.

So I said to the talent coordinator, "Listen, do I have to give my last line?"

"Well, how's the bandleader going to know when you're done?"

I said, "Well, I like to hear the laugh. How about if I just say, '*Thank you, thank you very much!*' Twice, okay? And that'll be the cue."

He agreed to this and went to tell the guys in the band. During the show, I waited backstage for my introduction from Dinah Shore. Finally, I heard her say, "Now we're going to bring out a very funny young man from Boston. He's got a unique brand of comedy. Please welcome, Mr. Jay Leno! Come out here, Jay!"

Because Dinah was such a warm presence, she tended to infect audiences with her own enthusiasm. And this audience took her lead and responded with a long, wonderful round of applause. It was almost unnatural. They even went, "Wooooo! Wooooo!"

I walked out, surprised and feeling like hot stuff.

I started with: "I'm from the United States! Are there any United States people here!"

This got a huge ovation—much more so than such a lame joke deserved.

So I said, "Oh! Thank you! Thank you very much!"

At which point, the bandleader looked up in a panic, threw down his magazine, stubbed out his cigarette—and started playing me off!

"BAAAA DAAAAH! BAAAAAM PAHHHH! BAAA BAAAHH! DAAAAAH! DAHHHHHN TAAAAAA!"

And I stood there, stunned.

Meanwhile, Dinah, who had been reading through her notes, looked up, smiled broadly, and started applauding. Which started the audience applauding wildly!

Now she was waving me over to her: "Come on over here, Jay! Come on over here!"

So I shrugged and walked over to her couch.

Still beaming, she said, "Sit right down! That's some of the freshest material I've heard in a long time!"

Was anybody paying attention here?

So I just sat down and said, "Well, thank you very much! At this rate, I could do this show eighty, ninety times a year!"

And, naturally, no one seemed to know what I was talking about. It was the most ridiculous shot of my career.

■　■　■

Of course, there was only one show that every comedian wanted to do. *The Tonight Show* was the Holy Grail. And it kept eluding me. I watched most of my peer group get their first shots on the show. Some of them exploded onto the national scene.

Some faded away. But at least they had gotten their chance. I waited and waited for mine. Every few weeks, the show's talent coordinators would drop into the comedy clubs to check out all of us. These visits were considered auditions. You knew they were there. And they knew you knew. On those nights, I would have my act down pat. But it didn't seem to matter. Very politely, I'd be told that I wasn't ready for the show quite yet.

And I understood their reasoning. There are basically two kinds of comedians: You have the strong attitude comics with no real jokes. And you have the joke comics with no performing skills or attitude. The ones who make it usually tend to be both. At the time, I was pretty good at being loud and sarcastic, saying things like: "Hey, that's great . . . *if you're a duck!*" Pure attitude. Amazingly, that sort of wiseacre stuff got big laughs, but you couldn't technically call them jokes. And this got to be a problem.

Harvey Korman, then Carol Burnett's right-hand comic foil, enjoyed coming to the clubs to watch the younger standups. One night, he brought Johnny Carson into the L.A. Improv specifically to see me and a few other comedians he liked. Of course, this sent an electric current through the place. Johnny was in the house! The mountain had come to us! It was thrilling and also a bit intimidating. But we all went up and did our acts, trying not to be self-conscious or, at least, not to look like idiots. On my way out, I approached their table and said to Johnny, "Thank you for coming in, sir."

And he said very genuinely, "That was funny stuff, but you're not quite ready. Your jokes are too far apart and you don't have enough of them. You're getting good laughs, but you need more jokes."

I wasn't going to hear it from any greater authority. I used to tell interviewers that I thanked him for the good advice, then went outside and egged his car. But, of course, I went outside and began thinking up jokes. For the next few months, I changed my act around and filled it with more jokes that had real payoffs.

Then, one night, Steve Martin wandered into The Comedy Store and saw me. He was just reaching his legendary peak as a standup—filling fifteen-thousand-seat arenas, wearing his white suit, changing comedy forever. He was already guest-hosting for Johnny, which was a pinnacle all its own. To us, he seemed like a kind of superhero. Whenever he came to the club to try out new stuff, comics packed the room to watch. But he would sometimes just hang around to see the rest of us. And, on this night, he caught me and said, "That was funny. I'm going to talk to *The Tonight Show* about you."

Which he must have done. Because the talent coordinators came right over to give me another look. And the next thing I knew, I was booked on the program. Johnny himself would be hosting. The date was set for March 2, 1977. Which, of course, I couldn't forget even if I wanted to.

This was going to be the moment of truth. Still, you didn't want to make yourself crazy worrying about it. But I was excited enough to go out and buy a videorecorder so that I could tape my shot. Technology being what it was in 1977, I paid *twelve hundred dollars* for a basic machine—an enormous JVC tape recorder. Completely incompatible with anything available now, it seemed to be steam-driven and made of cast iron. It weighed three hundred fifty pounds and—as best I could tell—was bulletproof. The most you could tape was a half-hour at a time. And the tapes were huge, the size of a human head. You'd load them in and hear *caaaa-chonnnnnk!* Then you'd press play and the lights would dim in the house. The belts on it would propel a Harley. Just a monstrosity. But, at least, I was now ready to record myself for posterity.

I called home to tell my parents and mentioned that Johnny's other guests that night would be Burt Reynolds and Diana Ross. My mother weighed in with her inimitable show business perspective: "You know," she said, "I don't know why they always go with those big stars. No one wants to see the big stars. They want to see *the new people.*"

I said, "Ma, I don't think anybody's really that anxious to see me."

"No, that's what people want! They're not interested in the big stars. You can see them anywhere! But where are you going to see *the new people?*"

On the big day, a handful of my comedian friends went to NBC's Burbank studios to provide moral support. (Contrary to popular opinion, whenever a comic does *The Tonight Show,* his contemporaries really do wish him well—and some even show up to help cheer and applaud.) Among the guys who came for me was Robin Williams. We'd gotten friendly at the clubs, where everyone was amazed by his energy. But he hadn't gotten his break yet. At one point that afternoon, I asked the *Tonight Show* talent coordinators, "Hey, what about this guy, Robin Williams?" They said, "We've seen him. He's all over the place! He runs around, never sits still. He doesn't really have jokes, he just kind of does odd things. We don't really think he'd be right for the show." Of course, within a year, he would be Mork from Ork and children would be playing with dolls in his likeness. (But—as an interesting footnote to my appearance on the show that night—if you ever see a tape, you can hear Robin's distinctively goofy *huh-huuuhh!* laugh in the background.)

I went to my dressing room and saw the little *Tonight Show* card on the door with my name printed on it, which I naturally stole afterward. For wardrobe, I chose the best suit I had, which happened to be bright green. Surprisingly, at the time, this was considered an attractive suit. It had been purchased for me to wear in *The Silver Bears*, which I did. Then again, in that movie, I was playing a gangster kid with bad taste. So who knows? Years later, the only thing that people remembered about my first appearance was the green suit. On his anniversary shows, Johnny would play the clip—which I came to call the *blackmail tape*—and unfailingly remark on my sartorial style. I was always secretly thrilled to be comic fodder for him. Once, he described the suit as "a used clown outfit." Another time, he said that I looked like an Italian elf.

Anyway, I suppose that I was feeling as green as that suit looked. Before the show, Johnny's executive producer, Fred De Cordova, took me aside to explain the ropes. He told me, "After you finish your set, whatever you do, don't move. Stay on your mark and look at me. If I move my hand this way, I'm waving you over to the couch. If I push away, that means just take a bow and go behind the curtain. But whatever you do— wait for my signal!"

"Yes, sir, Mr. De Cordova, fine."

And so, late in the program, after Burt Reynolds and Diana Ross had come out, I stepped through the curtain and did my first shot. I remember telling this joke: "Have you seen any of

David Janssen's commercials for Excedrin? That makes sense. *The man looks like a headache!*" That got a big laugh from Johnny—probably because he knew him. Anyway, it seemed to be going well. Then, a minute and a half into my set, I was heckled by somebody in the audience! Some guy actually shouted something at me. Out of the corner of my eye, I saw the staff panicking. And for a split second I froze. In all my years of telling jokes, hecklers were a staple. But this was *The Tonight Show!* This *never* happened. It was like being heckled in church!

So I just reverted to an old line that I used in clubs. I turned to Johnny and said, "This is the same kind of guy who talks to the TV at home . . . '*Look out, Kojak! Behind you!*' As if Kojak would tell him, "Oh, thank you, viewer! You saved my life!"

This got a huge reaction and really broke the ice. And, more important, Johnny seemed to like it. Which was one of those dream comedic rites of passage: Johnny's laugh of approval, the only music that really mattered.

I finished my set, the band played my outcue, I said, "Thank you!" And, doing exactly as I was told, I looked over at Fred De Cordova to find out where to go. And I saw him—*talking on the phone!* People were applauding. I kept staring at Fred—who now lit a cigarette and turned to speak with someone else!

What now?

I felt like I was dying! And the applause was fading! Telepathically, I was screaming to Fred, "*Heeeeeey! Help! What do I do? What do I do?*"

Now all of this happened over the course of maybe three seconds. But, to me, it might as well have been an hour and a half! Finally, Fred gave me a half-wave toward the desk. So I walked over and shook Johnny's hand. He gave me a big grin and also The Wink. Which was the greatest.

Oddly enough, I was more nervous watching it at home later that night. Somehow, that made the experience feel both more real and more nerve-racking. But maybe that had something to do with worrying about whether my monster tape recorder would brown out the neighborhood.

Over the next several months, I did *The Tonight Show* two or three more times. A couple of times, I got to sit on the couch next to Johnny, who was always very nice to me. During commercial breaks, he'd sometimes mention a joke that I'd told and say, "Hey, why don't you try the bit this way . . . Here's a line you could use." And he was always right.

But I soon realized that I'd made the classic mistake among comedians. My first shot had been a compilation of my very best material—and it had gone extremely well. The second shot was okay, not as funny—because I used the best of what I had left

I think Johnny's stunned by my bad lapels.

over. And the third shot, all in all, wasn't very good. The real trick is to get hot and then keep coming up with new stuff at this incredible pace. If you continue to take from the well, eventually the well runs dry. As mine seemed to do. My appearances just trailed off and I knew the inevitable. Back then, and even now, if you don't make that big smash with your first few shots, you've got to consider your options and try someplace else. For me, the best place seemed to be the road. If I couldn't get a nation's attention on television, I figured that I could do it one town at a time. And that would have to be my game plan.

■ ■ ■

An obvious stop was Las Vegas. In the past, I had opened in Lake Tahoe several times for John Denver and Johnny Mathis. But, for my Vegas debut, I would open for Tom Jones at Caesars Palace. In those days, Caesars never gave opening acts any billing, especially with big stars like Tom Jones. So my name wasn't on the marquee outside or anywhere else near the showroom. Which was fine. I was just happy to be working in the show business glitz capital.

My friend Budd Friedman, who runs The Improv, happened to be in town at the time and brought his wife over to visit me at the hotel. He asked me, "Any chance you can get us tickets for your opening show tonight?"

I said, "No problem, Budd! I'll get you in!"

There were always house seats available for performers to give away. So I led Budd and his wife through the Caesars lobby to the ticket office. Feeling kind of important, I said to the woman behind the window, "Hi, I'd like to get two tickets for tonight's show."

"I'm sorry, sir. The show's sold out."

I realized that the woman didn't recognize me.

I said, "Oh, I know. I'm Jay Leno, the opening act."

She frowned and said, "Mr. Jones does not have an opening act, sir."

"Yes, he does! I'm working with him."

"*I don't think so!*"

Now I looked like a complete idiot. And Budd was just reveling in this, stifling his laughter.

I said, "I am! I am! Look, can you find somebody . . ."

She turned to the woman at the next window and said, "Susan! Is there an opening act for Tom Jones?"

"*I don't think so!*"

"Are you sure?"

"Let me find out."

The first woman said, "Could you wait here, sir?"

At this point, tears were running down Budd's face. Finally, the other woman returned and said, "I guess there's some comic named Jackie Leon opening—"

"Fine! That's me! Two tickets, please!"

My first show that night went well and I felt pretty good about it. Just before Tom Jones ended his set, I walked through the showroom and out the main doors where the audience would shortly stream out. I figured this was my first time in Vegas and it'd be exciting to have people recognize me from the stage and toss me a few accolades. As I stepped into the lobby, an attractive girl flashed a big smile and said, "Hey, great show, huh?"

I said, "Oh, thanks, thanks!"

"How are you doing?"

"Oh, good, good."

"What are you doing now?"

"Oh, I'm gonna get a bite at the coffee shop."

"Really? Need any company?"

This was great! Vegas! I'd done my first show and now a beautiful woman wanted to be my entourage! I felt like Sinatra! So we sat down at the restaurant and talked a bit.

I said, "Where are you from?"

And she rolled her eyes and said, "Well, this chitchat is all very nice, but when are we going to get down to business?"

"Business? What business?"

"Well, it's two hundred dollars."

"What's two hundred dollars?"

She rolled her eyes again.

"Don't jerk me around! You pick me up, you know what this is all about!"

"No, I don't!"

Which, amazingly, I didn't.

She started yelling, "Oh, you asshole! You guys are all assholes!"

People were looking over at us and whispering.

"Fine, you asshole! Thanks for wasting my time!"

And she stomped out. As she passed the other tables, I distinctly heard people muttering "*Hooker . . . hooker . . . hooker.*" And I suddenly realized that she hadn't seen me onstage at all and had no idea who I was. She would have said, "Great show!" to *anybody* who came out of those doors!

Now I was this sleazeball comic picking up hookers. The worst part was overhearing a woman at the next table who looked just like my mom say, "And he looked like such a nice young man!"

12

I DON'T THINK THIS COMEDY THING IS GONNA WORK HERE

My life in comedy mystified my mother. For the longest time, she never quite understood what I did. She was especially puzzled by my constant road schedule. Until *The Tonight Show* became a full-time job, I spent more than two-thirds of every year playing one-nighters in every state of the nation. In the middle of one long tour, I stopped home to see my folks. I happened to overhear my mom on the telephone trying to explain to someone what it was that I was doing. She said, "Well, he has these little *skits* that he puts on from town to town."

Little skits? Like I was the vagabond village idiot, traveling to corners of the country, where I'd sit on a dunk tank and people threw apples at me! Of course, there were times as I crossed the map when she wasn't far from wrong.

For instance, there was a country-western club near Atlanta called the Rodeo Lounge that wanted to take a chance with comedy. I actually worked there in a *cage*. By cage, I mean that the stage was an enclosed chicken-wire box, which you entered through a chicken-wire door. I went inside, latched the door behind me, and started doing my act. This was the cue for drunken people to hurl glasses and beer bottles at the cage with all their might. The chicken wire would bend inward with every impact. I'd sort of dodge the incoming, trying to avoid being drenched in beer. And I'd keep doing my act, while guys screamed, "Hey, asshole! Sing! Sing!" And I realized that they had no idea what I was trying to do. More bottles hit. Then they would fill their mouths with whatever swill they were drinking and spit these putrid gushers at me through the wire! This was the only place I ever worked where it was necessary to towel off between jokes.

More madness: I once had a pickup date at a New Mexico bar that had an interesting division of clientele. On one side of the room, there sat several guys dressed in real cowboy attire, hats and all. On the other side were all American Indians. Like in some Old West saloon scene, they were split right down the middle, assembled to witness this so-called comedy night. I started my show and got a few laughs as I went along. Both sides of the room seemed to be with me. Then, after one joke, a cowboy pointed across the room and hollered, "That Injun's too stupid to get that one!"

An American Indian wearing a big stovepipe hat shot the cowboy a dirty look and hollered back, "Hey, you shut up!"

"Whatsa matter, redskin? I bet you didn't get that joke, either! Heh heh heh!"

Some other American Indians started yelling at the cowboy. And the other cowboys yelled right back at the Indians.

Suddenly, my act had touched off a range war! Barbs were

flying back and forth—which, of course, was preferable to bullets and flaming arrows. At least the West had evolved enough to let childish insults do the job. And they just kept on sparring.

"*Why don't you shut your mouth!*"

"*No, you shut your own mouth!*"

I said, "Hey, fellas! Take it easy! We can all work together here!" For the rest of the show, I felt like Dr. Quinn, Medicine Woman, out on a baby-sitting job! "Please, just stop it! Will you guys behave yourselves! Do I have to come out there and get wagons to circle you?"

After the show, the manager came over to me and said, "Thanks, but I don't think this comedy thing is gonna work here."

■　■　■

One of my earliest road gigs ever was at a strip joint in Minnesota, called the Mine Shaft. I was still living in Boston and, quite obviously, taking any job I could find. The Mine Shaft was remarkable in one way only: The place had no lights. The room was pitch-dark. Customers paid five bucks to get in and, for another five bucks, they would each get a genuine coal miner's hat, complete with a light on top of it. The lights would then fall on whatever the audience was looking at. Thus, whenever dancing girls came out, all of these coal miners' lights would fix upon the jiggling flesh.

I walked out to do my act: "Hey, everybody! How you doin'?"

I immediately realized that I couldn't even see the microphone in front of my face. I stood telling jokes in total darkness for the first three minutes!

The reason, of course, was that naked girls were still off dancing in corners. Nobody wanted to look at a comic onstage when that kind of option was available. Finally, the occasional person would glance over at me—probably to see who was distracting them from their drooling. So the bobbing hat lights would whip over to me, then whip away just as quickly. And each time this happened, I was instantly blinded by the flash of light! Then I'd go into horrible fits of squinting and blinking. I felt like I was being strobed by lasers. All in all, darkness was better.

■ ■ ■

The road is unforgiving. It's also endless. By the mid-seventies, comedy clubs were popping up in most cities, trying to cash in on the boom started by The Comedy Store and The Improv. Most of these gigs were fairly horrible. Audiences hadn't gotten the hang of actually *paying attention* to comics onstage. Often, I would come out to virtually no applause—much less to any remote sort of feigned interest. Usually, I'd begin by saying: "Well, what a wonderful ovation! You're just too kind. I can't handle it. So—good night!" Then I'd turn to leave, which usually got a laugh. Followed by some very fleeting attention. Followed by more disinterest.

At some indiscernible point, clubs started adopting truly ridiculous names that sounded more like Hostess snack cakes than nightspots. There were places called Ho-Ho's, Ha-Ha's, Hee-Hee's, Tickles, Giggles, Jokers, Zanies, and, my personal favorite, the Comeedie Inn. Sillier still were the "theme" clubs like the Comedy Boat, an actual floating barge whereupon if the acts didn't make you sick, the tossing of tides usually would.

The dumbest club of all—whose name now escapes me—
was located on a tiny island about one hundred yards offshore
on a Canadian lake. To get there, a kid would row out four people at a time in a small skiff. This wasn't so bad before shows,
but once the place closed for the night, bedlam broke loose on
the island. About a hundred people bolted outdoors like the
club was on fire, knocking one another down to get to the row-
boat! The kid would paddle furiously, island to shore, four people at a time, for the next three hours. Every night, he looked
like he'd been gripped by a new and agonizing hernia. Terrible
idea for a place.

Then there was the Comedy Deli, located in the hills of
West Virginia, big coal mining country. I played opening week
there, with an older black comedian who on different nights
identified himself as either Redd Foxx's brother or Flip
Wilson's cousin. Neither seemed to be true. He had the kind of
self-discriminatory act that black comics did in the fifties, just
to get work. One of his lines: "Ah'm not really *colored*! It's just
that the lights in here are very *bright*!" When the audience
applauded that line, I knew that I was in trouble.

Anyway, this place was an actual deli that had been con-
verted into a club. But no changes had been made to the place
other than the inclusion of a stage. There were no cocktail
tables and chairs—just the regular high-backed deli booths,
none of which faced the stage. So you couldn't actually see
anybody in the audience. And they could only see you by turning around and peeking over the tops of the booths.

I would look out at this creepy spectacle of disembodied
eyes peering back at me from the banquettes. It felt like the
children of the damned were ogling me. If there was any

laughter, it was muffled by the thick upholstery. In fact, the only thing I heard clearly was the horrible hacking coughs of the coal miners. Which registered on a seismic scale: "*Akaaaaaaahhaaaaa! Akaaaaaaaaahhaaaa!*" Just ear-shattering hemorrhaging—so loud that I couldn't even finish jokes! It sounded like a room full of heart attacks in progress. I kept thinking that I should get offstage and call for paramedics.

After the week, the manager became the second guy to tell me, "Thanks, son, but I don't think this comedy thing is gonna work here!"

■ ■ ■

On the road, I would find myself doing things that I'd *never* do at home. Blame it on stupefying boredom. For instance, no matter what small town I went through, I'd read *the whole newspaper*, section after section. More than once, I caught myself muttering, "Look at this! Tuna casserole with a graham cracker crust! Isn't that interesting!" Suddenly, I was clipping recipes from local Jaycee homemakers.

Without question, the worst part of the road life was killing time in daylight, waiting for night to fall when show-time came. My entire offstage existence seemed to revolve around watching television in whatever motel room I occupied. If I had to leave the room to do something, I'd gauge my activities by the *TV Guide* listings, which I read with religious fervor. (I always used to bring a copy of *TV Guide* with me onto the Letterman show to amuse Dave with the stupidest entries I found.) So it would be: Lunch at one o'clock; *Brady Bunch* at two; take a walk at three; *Three Stooges* at four. And, pathetically, so on.

But, for my money, nothing matched the sheer entertainment value of *The People's Court*, a program that spotlighted the most desperate displays of human pettiness ever broadcast. Next-door neighbors suing each other over possession of a garden hoe! I'll never forget the time a woman came to court with her hair in curlers. All I could think was: "Where is this woman going later? She was on national TV for the first time in her life! Did she have dinner plans with Gorbachev?"

But *The People's Court* saved my life on the road. Whenever it came on the air, I'd be so excited that I'd get up and do a little dance, which Mavis came to christen The Litigant. I now perform it almost nightly on *The Tonight Show*. It's the only dance I know. (By the way, it's *my dance*, so don't even think of suing me over it!)

My most memorable TV-watching incident on the road—and isn't it sad that there is one?—took place in Cherry Hill, New Jersey, where I was playing the Latin Casino. This was the kind of club that tended to attract an intimidating clientele, if you catch my drift. Even the management liked to create a sense of foreboding. Just to make sure you didn't ask for a raise, the owner would bring you into his office on the first day to show you his gun collection.

Anyway, I was put up for the week in a really cheap motor-court motel right off the highway, where you'd hear cars and trucks loudly whizzing past at all hours. Rooms cost six dollars a night, and the accommodations included ashtrays screwed to tabletops and televisions that had to be fed quarters in order to play. And a quarter would get you twenty minutes of programming. Which meant that you could never see any show in its entirety. Dramatic plots would always just hang in the air:

"And the murderer is—" *Bink!* And, naturally, there were no change machines in the place. I'd run down to the front desk, where they'd sneer and point to a sign: NO QUARTERS!

But that was the least of the peculiarities. The motel was all cinderblock, and each room was divided by a thin piece of plasterboard that didn't quite reach the ceiling or the floor. So there was an open space of about two inches at the top and bottom of the wall—exposing you to whatever was going on in the next room. One night, I was lying in bed, watching a quarter's worth of TV, when I heard a couple check into the room next door. I looked down at the floor and saw the toes of a pair of men's shoes slide through the open crack right into my room! Very creepy.

I tried not to think about it and kept watching TV. Suddenly, I heard a man's voice as though it was right next to me in my own room.

"Can you turn that down?"

I looked around mystified, then realized that the headboard of the couple's bed next door met the thin wall where my headboard was positioned. The voice came again, calm and even-toned.

"Uh, can you turn that down?"

"What?"

"Turn that TV down!"

So I lowered the volume to a barely audible setting.

"Turn it down a little more, please."

"Um, okay."

At this point, I was just looking at the pictures move. Whereupon the couple behind me started to have sex. Bedsprings were squeaking. Headboard was going *bang bang*

bang. I felt like I was in the room with them! Then the woman said, "I think that guy can hear us."

"No, he can't."

"Yes, he can."

"No, he can't!"

"YES, I CAN!"

Luckily, that seemed to kill the mood. They checked out about forty-five minutes later.

■　■　■

Worst lodgings ever: A club owner in Bakersfield didn't want to spring for motel accommodations. So he put comedians up in what he called his guest "condo." This was not a condo, but actually a two-car garage next to his house. He kept his car in one bay and he'd installed a bed in the other bay. I'd be sleeping at seven in the morning and, suddenly, the garage door would slowly screech open and his wife would walk in to get her car, which was right next to the bed. From under the covers, I'd look up and basically find myself on the street, as other cars drove by! The wife would tiptoe past me and say, "Oh, sorry." Then she'd start the engine, pull out, and the garage door would slowly tilt shut again. Very surreal way to sleep.

■　■　■

Strangest way I ever got a room: There was a motel next to the Front Row Theater in Cleveland. This place was situated so close to the expressway that when you stepped out of your room, you could be grazed by a speeding sideview mirror. One night, I got to town and went to check in. The woman at the desk said, "I'm sorry. We're all booked up." I explained that there had to be a room held under my name, as arranged by the theater. She looked again and said there was nothing. From the back, I heard a loud ruckus. A man was screaming, *"Get out and stay out!"* It was the manager, and he was evicting the rock star Stephen Stills! Down the hallway came Stephen, looking rumpled and forlorn. He glanced up at me and casually said, "Hey, Jay." I said, "Hey, Stephen." And he slunk out the door, hauling a couple of bags. At which point, the woman behind the desk said, "Oh, I think something just opened up."

■ ■ ■

Oddest media request on the road: I was working in Reno with Tony Orlando and got a call from a local TV station. The anchorwoman said she had an idea for a news feature and wanted me to be part of it. I told her to come by, which she did, and I asked, "So what's the story?" She said, "Well, we're doing a story on celebrity loneliness, and since you're on the road so much, we thought you'd have a lot to say about it." *Celebrity loneliness?* I thought, "Aren't there more pressing problems in the world to be investigated on the news?" So I had to decline. But I told her, "Talk to Tony Orlando. He'll talk about it. Ever since the girls in Dawn left him, he's never been the same, you know."

■ ■ ■

Reno was always a strange place to work. The shops in town sold the most ridiculous gift merchandise. Not that I'm any kind of tastemaker, but you have to wonder about any place that would sell sterling silver ashtrays in the shape of human buttocks with the inscription: PARK YER BUTTS HERE! I remember seeing a twelve-thousand-dollar solid gold statue of a man holding a barrel around his torso. And when you pulled down the barrel, the man would pee on you. Just lovely conversation pieces!

In this questionable environment, I once went looking for a birthday present for my mother. I found a pawnshop, thinking it might at least have some antiques for sale. I explained the situation to the guy at the counter.

He asked, "How old of a woman is she?"

"Seventy-two."

He said, "Hmmm. How about this?"

And he pulled out a pearl-handled derringer.

I said, "I don't really think she wants a gun."

He said, "Oh, but it's a woman's gun! See the inlaid pearl there. All handcrafted. Really, you should think about it. She'll love it!"

He was completely serious.

I tried to reason with him: "Well, it's only a single shot. What if she missed? She couldn't reload before someone returned fire."

The guy stroked his chin, deep in thought, then said, "I understand. Good point. How about a little larger handgun that holds six or eight bullets?"

"Well, I don't think that it would fit in her purse."

"Of course, of course. I know! How about something in a repeating rifle?"

"I don't want to get her a repeating rifle! Maybe I'll look for something else. You know, it's been a long time since she last got into a shoot-out with the baker."

▪ ▪ ▪

One of my first out-of-town gigs was at the famous Chicago club Mister Kellys. I opened for the singer Freda Payne, who had the big hit "Band of Gold." When I reached town, the entertainment director came to see me at my hotel. He said, "Listen, before you come to the club tonight, I wanted to tell you that we've got a little problem with the marquee. We ran out of E's."

"What do you mean you're out of E's?"

He said, "We've only got two E's and Freda Payne used up both of them."

"So what are you saying?"

"Well, on the sign out front, you're JAY L NO."

"JAY L NO?"

"Look, nobody's gonna notice. Don't worry."

My favorite marquee in Chicago.

So that night, I was billed as JAY L NO and the show went well, anyway. In fact, the review in the Chicago paper the next day was quite complimentary: "Mr. No is a bright young comedian who opened the show for Miss Payne . . ."

■ ■ ■

I was once hired to play the ballroom of an old hotel in Ogunquit, Maine. Very conscientiously, they called ahead to ask if I needed anything special in order to perform. I said no. They said, "Do you want an opening act?" I said, "No, my act is well over an hour long. That's okay." I arrived at the hotel about a half-hour before the show. And, as always, I asked, "How's the sound system?"

The guy looked at me, puzzled, and said, "Well, you *brought* the sound system, right?"

"No! I don't have a sound system!"

"Well, we asked you if you needed anything!"

"I assumed that you'd have a *microphone* . . ."

"No, no. This hotel was built in the 1800s! We don't have any sound systems!"

"But you've got a nightclub here!"

"It's a *ballroom*—not a nightclub! We're just trying a comedy night."

So I had to stand on the stage of this cavernous ballroom—and *shout*.

"HOW ARE YOU DOIN'! ANYBODY BEEN TO MCDONALD'S?"

People were yelling back: "WHAT? WE CAN'T HEAR!"

So I tried a different tack. I went down and walked among the crowd, telling my jokes. Which caused people on the other side of the ballroom to get up and come over to where I was.

They kept yelling, "WHAT? WHAT?"

"I SAAAIIID, HAVE YOU EVER BEEN TO MCDON-AAAALLLDDD'S?"

Afterward, the hotel guy came over and said, "You know, I don't think this comedy thing is gonna work here."

■   ■   ■

Variation on the same desperate theme: Early on, I went down to George Washington University to open for the group Rare Earth. The stage was set up in a gymnasium. There were no chairs for the audience, which was composed mostly of surly teenage boys. So they all just stood around, loitering like punks. Before the show, I approached the manager of the stage crew and said, "Hi, I'm the opening act."

"Yeah, right."

He couldn't have cared less.

I asked, "Which mike do you want me to use?"

"You can't use any of them. We've got expensive equipment here, buddy."

"Well, I've got to use *something*."

"I don't care. You're not using any of our stuff! And you can't get onto the stage, either. Everything's set up for our guys and you can't screw it up."

"I can't get on the stage?"

"No!"

Then the event promoter took me aside and repeated, "They don't want you onstage. You're gonna have to work down on the gym floor."

"But the audience is standing there! And I'll be right in the middle of them!"

"That's right."

Finally, somebody wangled me a microphone with an extralong cord that snaked down onto the gym floor. There wasn't even a box for me to stand on. So I walked out, bumping into all these teenagers, and faced them eye-to-eye to start the show. I said, "Hey, everybody! How you doing? I'm opening the show! Anybody here from Boston?"

Suddenly, I sensed trouble coming. The next thing I knew, somebody grabbed the mike wire and jerked it hard. The mike flew out of my hand and straight into the crowd. I screamed, "Hey, give me that!" Frantically, I ducked down and tried to chase the mike through their legs.

Then I heard some kid's voice booming over the speakers, trying to impress his friends: "Hey, Billy, you suck! Hey, Larry, you're an asshole! Ha ha ha!"

Finally, I found the wire and followed it to the end, where the mike had been ripped loose and, of course, stolen! My act was finished before it had begun.

Not only was I not paid—I got charged seventy-five bucks for the missing microphone. I was told by the promoter, "You're a professional! You should be able to hang on to your equipment!"

■ ■ ■

I played the Cellar Door in Washington for a week, opening for Muddy Waters, the great blues guitarist. Usually, blues and comedy are a pretty good mix. Usually. On the first night, I wasn't onstage for more than a minute when, from the corner of my eye, I spotted a large menacing guy off to the side. He looked angry and seemed to be sidling toward the stage. But I didn't give him much thought and began telling another joke—*when I felt the guy onstage right behind me*. I turned just as he brought a Heinz ketchup bottle down on my head! *Bonnkkk!* As I went down, I heard the audience cheer! *"Yeah! Woooooo!"* Then I was out cold.

When I woke up, the back of my head was shaved and I had eight stitches. Worse yet, I was docked a night's pay because, according to the owner, as a "professional comedian," I should be ready for things like this to happen. Once again, I realized that all good comedians should travel with a cut man.

■ ■ ■

Oklahoma! Where the comic came sweepin' down the plain! So many unforgettable images to recall:

Going through Oklahoma City, I asked somebody for a restaurant recommendation. He said, "Hey, aren't you Eye-talian? We've got one of the best Eye-talian restaurants here! In fact, the owner's from Iowa!" I went there and saw the red-checked tablecloths and wine bottles along the wall. All of which looked promising. I ordered spaghetti and meatballs. Then the waiter asked, "You want fries with that? It comes with fries, you know." So I got the fries, plus three slices of Wonder Bread for sopping marinara. As they say, "When in Oklahoma City, do as the Romans do!"

(This, by the way, was vastly preferable to a place in West Virginia, where the menu listed something called a Wop Salad. The waiter there explained that it was a regular salad made with Italian dressing. I said, "Oh, of course! How foolish of me not to know that!" Then there was the old diner in Des Moines that hung signs boasting: PIZZA—THE NEWEST TASTE TREAT! YOU CAN EAT IT WITH YOUR HANDS!)

Another great Oklahoma spectacle was the church row you found in most towns. All along these thoroughfares, church after church would have marquees announcing the sermon of the day. And, in the tradition of that Old-Time Religion, every church would try to top the next one with a stunning billing:

EX-BIKER TALKS ABOUT HIS LIFE WITH THE GANG AND HIS RETURN RIDE TO CHRIST!

Then another hundred yards down:

EX-PROSTITUTE TELLS HOW SHE FINALLY WOUND UP IN BED WITH THE LORD!

This was like daytime television with preachers presiding instead of Ricki Lake and Geraldo!

But I got an even better sense of regional piety in Tulsa. I was playing an old auditorium, where the audience was very nice and receptive. Not long after starting my act, I noticed that a man in the front row seemed to have something written in chalk on the sole of his shoe. I couldn't make out what it said, so I ignored it.

I went on with my material. Then I saw another guy with something scrawled on his shoe. I thought, "What *is* that?" This was getting peculiar. So, as I walked the stage, I made an effort to look at everyone's shoes. I'd say that four out of five people had something written on their shoes! All in white chalk. And I couldn't figure out what it was.

Afterward, I found the local promoter and asked him about it. He nodded and said, "Oh, yes, yes. That's Satan."

"What do you mean it's *Satan?*"

He said, "We have a preacher here in town and he tells his parishioners to write *Satan* on the bottom of their shoes with chalk. That way, when they walk around, they'll be stomping him out."

And I said, "Oh, of course! That makes sense."

I had been staring at a sea of Satans!

Although I guess it was sort of flattering. If you're going to see Satan anywhere in Oklahoma, it was great to know that it would be at my show!

13

WHY DON'T YOU WAKE HER THE HELL UP, PAL?

And then, one time, the view from the stage changed my life. In January 1976, I stood onstage at The Comedy Store and saw Mavis. Mavis Nicholson. Dark, attractive, intelligent-looking, and she even laughed in the right places. But there was something different going on here. I knew that I had to meet her. In those days, comedians had one surefire way of accomplishing that goal. You would hang around outside the women's bathroom. If you waited there long enough, every woman would eventually pass through the portals. So I loitered there and, as true romance would have it, that's where we met. I believe I asked her out and I believe she accepted and, after a short while, there wasn't a point that she wasn't part of my life, sharing all the great and stupid adventures and helping me to make sense of them.

We were, and are, opposites in most every way. Which I love. There's a better balance. At the time we met, Mavis did write comedy, but our worlds would diverge from there on. She was raised in Los Angeles, the product of a quirky, kind of eccentric family. Her father, Nick Nicholson, was a fun-loving character actor whose face turned up in all kinds of TV shows and movies. (Then again, he also played the hooded executioner in the film *In Cold Blood*.) And, as different upbringings tend to dictate, her qualities are ones that I lack.

I don't consider myself to have much of a spiritual side, but Mavis almost has a sixth sense about people and situations. She has deep focus, and I fly off in twenty directions at once. She reads fifteen books a week, mostly classic literature. I collect classic car and motorcycle books. She loves European travel; I don't want to go anywhere people won't understand my jokes. She can throw out old stuff; I save everything. I have my cars and bikes and garage; Mavis has no mechanical ability whatsoever and wouldn't begin to know how to use a screwdriver. But, most important, she exposes me to things and ideas that never would have otherwise come my way. We each handle our separate realms and work as a genuine team.

From the start, those realms could nicely intersect: For instance, the first place we ever made love was in the backseat of my 1955 Buick Roadmaster. After moving to Los Angeles, I answered a newspaper ad and bought it for three hundred fifty bucks. When I had no place else to stay, I often slept in it. A very roomy car, it could seat seven—*for dinner*. I used to say that it didn't have a radio, so I'd bring in live acts. Anyway, I still have it parked in my yard. I would never sell it, for obvious sentimental reasons.

■ ■ ■

Eventually, Mavis and I moved in together, which seemed kind of preordained. Odd as it sounds, every woman I had ever lived with was born on the same day. Or, at least, within the same twenty-four-hour calendar period. September 5 and 6. Mavis was born on the fifth. This is nothing that I ever sought out. I'm no great believer—or disbeliever—in the fateful order of things. It just seemed to always happen that way and I accepted it at face value. Women born on that day have some kind of magnetic force that affects me like gravity.

Once, several years ago on *The Tonight Show*, I was interviewing the cartoonist Cathy Guisewite, who draws the comic strip *Cathy*, and I recognized a certain spark about her. During a commercial break, I leaned over and said, "I don't mean this as a pass. Please don't misinterpret, but I find you interesting and attractive. What's your birthday?" And, of course, it was September 6. I wonder what Beyondo would make of all this?

The only problem living together presented was how my mother reacted to it. She never actually objected, but she had a way of dropping hints of disapproval. I would take Mavis home to visit my parents and have dinner.

I'd say something like, "Pass the milk, Mom."

And she'd mutter, "You don't buy the cow if you get the milk for free . . ."

"What, Mom?"

"Nothing."

"Can you pass the bread, Mom?"

"What's another slice off the loaf, hmmm?"

"What, Mom?"

"Oh, nothing, nothing . . ."

I remember the first time I fully understood her feelings

about men and women cohabiting out of wedlock. I was thirteen, and most every Saturday I would go to the Andover
Playhouse with my buddies to see a movie. We'd see everything from *The Three Stooges in Orbit* to *Spartacus*. One week,
they were showing a funny Jack Lemmon movie called *Under
the Yum Yum Tree*. I told my mom that I was thinking of going
to see it. She made a few calls on the neighborhood Mom
Information Exchange Network. Then she came back and told
me, "You're not seeing that movie!"

"Why?"

"You're not seeing that movie!"

This was why: *Under the Yum Yum Tree* was a sex comedy—
G-rated by today's standards—in which Jack Lemmon played a
love-crazed landlord obsessed with one of his tenants, Carol
Lynley, who was *actually living with her fiancé*, Dean Jones.
Without ever sleeping with him, she wanted to find out what
being married would be like.

My mother thought that this was just *scandalous*! Jack
Lemmon had always seemed so nice—and now he was doing
this *porno movie*! She actually got together with some other
moms and called the theater to complain. And she never
forgot. Even as recently as about eight years ago, when my
parents were staying with me, I flipped on the TV and found
Under the Yum Yum Tree playing. I said, "Hey, Mom, look
what's on!"

"We're not watching that!"

To this day, I've never seen the movie. Of course, my
mother was a very conservative woman. Which made it more
fun to tease her about sex. Years later, long after Mavis and I
were married, I sat down with her and said, "Mom, let me ask

you something. Did you and Dad ever, you know, *do anything* before you got married?"

"*Never mind what we did!*"

I said, "Ma! I'm married! I'm in my thirties! We're just talking!"

"*Never mind! It was a different time then!*"

"What was different?"

"*Never mind! People were different then and times were different!*"

"Does that mean yes?"

"*No, it does not mean yes!*"

I never could quite get a straight answer. But then I remember being home from college one day when I heard my mother whisper to my father, "I understand that the couple down the street are getting a d-i-v-o-r-c-e."

I hollered, "Ma! I'm in college! I know how to spell *divorce*! You don't have to whisper it! I know what it means!"

"Oh, you're so grown-up!"

■ ■ ■

Mavis went everywhere on the road with me. She was game for all the glamour that my life in show business afforded. Which was none. In the early days, we'd stay in these horrible comedy condos with the prestained beds. The sheets were never changed from comedian to comedian. This was especially disgusting if you knew some of the guys who came through ahead of you.

I once played two weeks at Rodney Dangerfield's club back in New York—although I don't think Rodney had a financial interest in the place any longer then. Anyway, for the duration

Mavis and I got married on the same day as my parents—November 30. That worked for them for fifty-seven years and it seems to be working for us, too.

of the gig, Mavis and I lived in a windowless storage room at the back of the club. Actually, it was more of a walk-in closet with a refrigerator and a mattress on the floor. The only light was a blinding naked hundred-watt bulb dangling from a string overhead. Otherwise, it was pitch-dark. Mavis hated it, but there we were, two for the road.

Very early on, no matter the venue, we agreed that it was probably best if she didn't sit in the audiences of my shows. She would always help me with my material and offer suggestions. But making a significant other watch every show is a terrible idea. Comics do this all the time with new girlfriends and it inevitably backfires in the funniest way. At the beginning, he'll bring her to his show—and consider it a date! Of course, the first time a woman sees your act, she's fascinated, she laughs. The second time, she thinks, "Didn't I hear this stuff before?" The third time, she thinks, "It's the exact same act!"

By the fourth time, she looks around and thinks, "Why are these idiots laughing? I hate this material!" After that, she begins to take on the look of an abused dog and will sit there seething.

So we bypassed that torture. Plus, there were other ways to make Mavis mad at me—although she always resisted some obvious temptations to do so. Life with a comedian isn't for everybody. You're so immersed in your career that everything else takes a backseat, even people sometimes. Most normal people who get involved with comedians, male or female, ultimately become jealous of your act. Unless perhaps your mate is also in the business. But that never seems to work, either. Two performers in one house requires twice the patience, maybe much more.

But, from the start, Mavis has been the picture of patience. Somehow she knew that, until I got rolling, the comedy had to be the all-consuming passion. Plus, I wasn't going anywhere. I wasn't seeing anyone else. I knew comedians whose spouses or mates tried to test them, dare them not to work. When forced to make that choice, they're not going to be happy. You have to work. You cannot not work. Me, especially. And Mavis always understood that. Which only made me love her more. And, in some ways, it's even better now than when we first got married.

Of course, the story of how we got married is almost as romantic as the story of how we met. We'd been together for about four years, during which time she expressed no interest in marriage. She expressed more interest in *not* getting married. Then, one day, I realized that I had a bunch of insurance policies that covered me for everything. But Mavis had no insurance of any kind. If she got sick or was in an automobile accident, she wouldn't be covered at all. Unless she was my wife, that is. So I told her that I thought we should get married. And she agreed. Which my mother thought was the funniest thing she ever heard: "Oh, they got married because he had some policy! Mr. Cheapskate! Mr. Skinflint!"

Funny thing was, I got my practical side from her. And Dad, after all, sold insurance policies for most of his life. I had to pick up a *little* of his salesmanship *somewhere* along the way.

■   ■   ■

Mavis had heard my stories about some of the mob guys connected with East Coast showplaces. But it wasn't until I brought her back there for the first time that she got a close-up look. I was working at an upstate New York theater that was alleged to have direct ties with Jimmy "The Weasel" Fratianno. At the airport, we were picked up by two huge palookas in dark suits and sunglasses. One said, "Mr. Leenos, I'm Rocko and this is Vincent. We're here to take youse and your lovely wife to the theater. Will you please get into the automobile. And, please, Mr. Leenos, if there's anything that you desire, we will take care of it."

We got in the backseat and Mavis had panic in her eyes. She whispered, "Gee, these guys look like the real thing!"

So I teased, "If we go into the city, honey, I may need to pack a rod, so don't be alarmed."

I hadn't realized that the guys in front could hear me. But the one in the passenger seat turned and said, "You need a rod, Mr. Leenos? No problem."

And from his coat he took out a gun and passed it to me in the backseat.

"You can take this here. It's got no numbers on it or nothin', so don't worry. If you wanna keep it for your stay here, please feel free!"

Of course, Mavis's eyes were bugging out at this point.

I said, "No, no, I was just kidding. I don't really need a gun."

"No, please, Mr. Leenos! We insist. Please take it with you and use it in good health."

I said, "No, no. I was just teasing my wife. I don't really need it. I'm fine."

"Okay, but it's not a problem if you want to hang on to it."

"No, no. Thanks, guys. That's very nice of you, though."

■ ■ ■

Once I had a three-day gig in New Orleans, and Mavis had always wanted to go there. But I was back East and she was in Los Angeles. So we arranged to fly in the same afternoon and meet at the airport. Her plane would get in at 2:30 and mine would arrive at 2:45. I said, "Just wait at your gate. As soon as I get in, I'll meet you there." So I landed, ran down to her gate, and nobody was there. Then I ran back to my gate and she wasn't there, either. I ran back to her gate once more and asked what time the plane had arrived.

The counterperson said, "Oh, it got in about an hour early."

So where was she? I started to run back toward my gate again and saw a couple of airport cops whom I'd run past three times already. I thought maybe they'd know where I should go to look for Mavis. They seemed to recognize me.

"Hey, you're that Jay Leena!"

"Yeah, yeah, how you doing? Nice to meet you. I was supposed to meet my wife and I know she's around here somewhere and I just can't find her. Is there some kind of a main waiting area?"

They sent me down to another waiting area, but she wasn't there. I returned to the cops.

"Well, are you sure she was on the plane, Mr. Leena?"

I said, "Yeah, I'm sure or else she would have told me. I was supposed to meet her right here."

They exchanged a kind of knowing look.

I said, "Is there something wrong?"

"Well, Mr. Leena, it has nothing to do with you. But, you know, a lot of times women come to a city like New Orleans, they see those bright lights, and they *just run off!*"

I said, "Oh, I don't think she's *run off.*"

"Well, again, I'm not questioning your relationship or nothing. But sometimes, women come to town, get all worked up, and just run off!"

I said, "I'm sure she hasn't run off."

"All right, Mr. Leena. Good luck! We hope you find her."

Then they shook their heads and chuckled a bit. Like I'd been ditched at the airport!

I found her in the coffee shop, but I couldn't leave without showing Toody and Muldoon that my wife hadn't run off with Doug Kershaw into the Cajun Bushland!

So I walked Mavis over to them.

"Here she is, you guys! I found her!"

"Okay, Mr. Leena! You just hold on to her tight now!"

■ ■ ■

Not that I haven't had a scare in that department: Since I'm not much on foreign travel, Mavis likes to take her mother on trips abroad. I always have her itinerary and, time differences being what they are, I tend to call her very late to see how they're doing. Once when they were in Paris, I called her hotel at about two in the morning.

The hotel operator answered: "*Bonjour!*"

"Mavis Leno, please?"

They put the call through—and *a Frenchman answered!*

"*Allô?*"

I said, "Oh, I'm sorry. I have the wrong room. Sorry to bother you."

So I called the hotel back and said, "I'm sorry, but you put me through to the wrong room. It's Leno. L-e-n-o. Leno. Mavis Leno."

They double-checked and rang the room for me.

"*Allô?*"

It was the same guy!

I said, "I'm terribly sorry. I'm calling for Mrs. Leno and they keep giving me the wrong room."

"Yes, Meesus Leno eez here, but she's asleep."

SHE'S ASLEEP?!

I said, "*Oh, she's asleep, huh? Why don't you wake her the hell up, pal?*"

And he hung up on me!

Now I was going crazy. I called back and told the operator, "Leno, please!"

"*Allô! Leno?*"

"Yes, put Mrs. Leno on!"

"No, she eez asleep!"

I said, "Just put her on the goddamn phone!"

Then I heard French gibberish and finally she came to the phone.

"*Allô?*"

It didn't sound like her.

"Mavis?"

"*Pardon?*"

"Mrs. Leno?"

"Yes, but theese eez not the same . . ."

It was another guy named Leno and his wife! I'd never met a Leno anywhere who wasn't my relative! Now I found two French Lenos staying in the same place as my wife. Finally, I got Mavis on the phone. She couldn't understand why I sounded so annoyed. This is exactly why I don't like to leave the country.

■ ■ ■

A few years ago, I had a weekend job out of town. As always when packing for a quick trip, I reached into my drawer and grabbed a bunch of socks and a couple changes of underwear, then pulled out two suits and was off to the gig. I returned a couple days later, and Mavis came in to ask me about the trip as I was unpacking.

"It was all right, it was a fun gig, blah blah . . ."

While I was talking to her, I looked down into my hand and saw a pair of black panties! *How did these get into my suitcase?* I realized that Mavis doesn't have any black panties. I had no idea where they came from, but I did know that this looked more than a little bit incriminating. Which was ridiculous. *I didn't do anything!*

225

So, before Mavis could see, I quickly grabbed the panties and crunched them up in my fist. Then when she turned her back, I threw them on top of a tall clothes chest. We walked out of the room, but I knew I had to go back and get rid of them. I waited for her to go to the bathroom. Then I stole back, grabbed them, ran outside, and put them in an empty motor oil can. I put the cap on it, then buried the can in the trash under a pile of garbage. I still couldn't figure out what this was all about, but at least the evidence was gone.

A couple days later, Mavis said to me, "Would you look in your sock drawer? I got a pair of black panties last week at Patti's shower as a party favor, and I think they might have gotten mixed up with your socks. I can't find them anywhere!"

Uh-oh.

How to explain this? Better not even try.

"Gee, honey, there's nothing in here but socks! Sorry."

■ ■ ■

We bought our first house in Nichols Canyon, part of the Hollywood Hills. It was customary where I grew up to go meet your neighbors when you moved onto the block. I told Mavis that we should do the friendly thing and try that here. She pointed out that life in Hollywood wasn't the same as life back East, but agreed to go along with me. So I went out and actually bought a cake to give them, which I thought was a nice touch. Then we walked over to the house across the way. We rang the doorbell, and a man wearing a bathrobe and sunglasses answered.

He said, "Yes?"

I said, "Hi, we're your new neighbors across the street."

He closed his robe a little, and I realized that he was naked underneath.

"Uh, yes?"

"We just moved in and wanted to say hello. We've got a cake for you!"

Suddenly, I felt like Goober. I stepped forward to give him the cake and, beyond the door, I saw his all-white living room ablaze with thousand-watt kleig lights. A little strange.

He looked at me, confused. "A cake?"

"Yes, it's a cake. A gift."

A woman's voice from inside the house said, "*Cake? Bring in the cake!*"

So we walked in and saw on the floor two naked women who'd pulled throw rugs over their bodies. And then we saw another guy in bikini briefs behind a camera.

Then it occurred to me: *They're shooting a porno movie!*

The man in the robe handed the cake to the women, who pounced on it: "Oh, a cake! Thank you!"

Mavis and I looked at each other and shrugged.

I cleared my throat and said, "Um, hi. We're the Lenos, your neighbors . . ."

The guy in the robe said, "Uh, great. Nice meeting you."

Feeling like complete idiots, we gave a little wave and left. These people clearly thought we were the biggest rubes in the world. As the door closed behind us, we heard:

"Who the hell was that?"

"Just some jerk who bought a house."

"Think he knew what was going on?"

"Nah, he looked too stupid."

For some reason, I didn't learn from that experience.

Because when we moved several years later to Beverly Hills—
a place where you rarely if ever see your neighbors—I did it
again. Given the change of economic strata, I thought we
should bring a bottle of champagne next door this time and
introduce ourselves. So we walked over.

Bing bong!

A maid came to the door.

"Hi, we're your new neighbors!"

"I'm sorry, but Mr. and Mrs. So-and-So aren't home right
now."

I handed her the champagne anyway, and told her to pass
it on with our compliments.

She said, "By the way, are you keeping a full staff or a half
staff?"

I had no idea what she was talking about.

Mavis whispered to me, "Maids, butlers."

So I sort of swaggered a bit and said, "Oh, I don't know.
Probably a half." Like we'd ever have a staff!

We went back home. A few days later, a note arrived from
next door, which said, "Thank you, but in the future please do
not give the help liquor." We still haven't met those neighbors.

■ ■ ■

Mavis had a wonderful, goofy old cat called Moomin who lived
to be about fifteen. Then she just sort of wore out. When she
died, we wrapped her in a big plastic bag and buried her in the
backyard of the Nichols Canyon house, even marked the spot
with a little cross. This seemed like an appropriate final resting
place for Moomin.

Unfortunately, not long afterward, the time came for us to

move to a larger house. We put our place on the L.A. market, which had become overrun with speculators who loved knocking down old things and building new monstrosities. Because we'd invested a lot of love and hard work into the house, I wanted to make sure we sold to someone who appreciated what we'd done. I turned away several speculators, until a woman looked at the place and crowed, "Oh, I love this house! I'd love to buy this house! I'm a single woman and this is just perfect for me."

We had a good feeling about her, so we said, "okay, it's yours." We told her that we'd clean the rugs and have the house in sparkling condition for her. She said, "Oh, gee, that would be great! But you really don't have to!" But it just seemed like the right thing to do. So, the week before moving, we rented steam cleaners and did all the carpets. Mavis went after every little windowpane with the Windex. We got the place in terrific shape.

The woman was going to be taking possession on a Saturday, so we got all our stuff out and moved into our new house. That Thursday I had to leave town for a gig and wouldn't be back until late Friday night. While I was gone, Mavis called to tell me that the woman had people coming to dig up part of the backyard on Saturday morning because of some plumbing situation.

I said, "Uh-huh . . ."

"But the cat's buried back there!"

"I know."

"We have to move the cat! We have to bury her at the new house!"

"What?!"

But, of course, that's exactly what I did. I got home from the airport and went back to the Nichols Canyon place at midnight. Always a perfect hour for grave robbing. I thought that I had a shovel in the car trunk. But, naturally, I didn't. The only thing I could find was a kitchen spoon. So, like a crazed Boy Scout, I started to dig up Moomin with Oneida flatware. An hour later, I found her, still wrapped in plastic, although it was wearing thin. She'd been dead for a few months and the stench was just unbearable!

I took the plastic bag and laid it on the car seat next to me. Then I headed home. As I drove down the hill, however, I hit the brakes too suddenly. Everything in the car lunged forward. Including the bag. Which crashed to the floor and split open.

Oh, the dead-cat stench!

Now it was toxic. I couldn't breathe. I opened the sun roof, stuck my head out the window, and coughed to the point of hemorrhaging. I thought I was choking to death!

Finally, I got to our new house in Beverly Hills. But since we'd just moved in, I had no idea where we'd packed the garden tools. Still no shovel. Worse yet, the property here had been built on rock. So, once again, I used my grave-digging spoon—along with a knife, this time—and began chipping away at the solid ground, like some lifer trying to bust his way out of Sing-Sing.

It was four in the morning before I finally got the cat buried.

The next day, Mavis and I drove back to the old house to see what was going on with the backyard. When we pulled up, we saw a huge bulldozer roll off a truck out front. I thought, "Why would they need a bulldozer to dig up some water pipes?"

Unless . . .

We sat there and watched it happen: The bulldozer just plowed directly into the house and crushed it flat! Boom! Clean carpets and shiny windows and everything. Gone like that. All that was left standing were two fireplaces and a chimney. The woman turned out to be just another speculating developer.

At least we got the dead cat out.

14

THE $18,000 SUIT

At some point, people started recognizing me, which is both an odd and a gratifying phenomenon. It began happening more and more sometime during 1982, the year *Late Night with David Letterman* debuted on NBC. Over the next several years, Dave would have me on his show once every six weeks or so. I would come in from the road, sit down next to him, and try to entertain him with all kinds of mock outrage about stuff that struck me as stupid. Those shots were the most fun that I'd ever had on television. Having grown up in New England, I felt that doing the other talk shows required a certain sense of decorum. Whether it was Johnny or Merv or Mike, these were all *adult* men, all my elders, which limited my urge to be a wise-guy comedian with them. For the longest time, for instance, I didn't know whether to address Johnny as Mr. Carson or sir.

But Dave's was the first show on which I felt that I could really just be me. We were peers. Everyone who worked for him was our age—or even younger. Plus, I always knew how to make Dave laugh. Years later, I learned that the best way to make Johnny laugh was to tell stories about real people, family, and relationships. He had that bedrock midwestern sensibility and seemed to like to hear about my parents. But on the Letterman show, I could suddenly use the kind of odd turns of phrase and peculiar imagery that wouldn't have made much sense on *The Tonight Show*.

I remember once telling Dave about my irrational fear of circuses: "It's a traveling syphilitic side show! Diseased animals and hermaphrodite clowns throwing anthrax spores at the children . . . This is like entertainment from the ninth century! Geeks, trolls, mutants, all these inbred circus people . . . They come out from under bridges, releasing disease and pestilence into the air. I don't like the circus."

Dave said, "But the kids like it."

"Yeah, well, I guess if the *kids* like it . . ."

Dave and I could tease each other. He knew when I pulled out old material that he'd heard me do years earlier at The Comedy Store. He'd laugh less at the joke than at the idea that I was desperately reaching so far back. To get me on to the subject of current events, he'd always say, "What about the news? I know you're a big *fan* of the news!" Which always killed me. Or to launch me into some fit of bombast, he'd usually ask: "So—do you have any beefs this time out? Anything that's stuck in your craw? Gnawing at you? Eating at you?" This became known as the What's Your Beef segment, which I loved to do, because I'd get all riled up, which seemed to entertain Dave.

My favorite way to drive him batty was to bring food onto

the show and eat it all through my segment. He could never understand how I could eat on television. Of course, I've always loved to eat while I'm doing something else. So this was perfect for me! I'd try to get him to eat with me, but he'd never go for it. So I would just chomp on and mystify him. Like the night I brought out a sack of greasy gyros:

Dave: I'm sorry, did I catch you with a mouthful of food?
  Me: Hey, I'm on the go! Try one!
Dave: Maybe when I don't have an audience to talk to—then
      I'll have my meal!
  Me: (*Eating, talking.*) Mmmpphhhnnfffnnggggghhhh.
Dave: Let me ask you something: You didn't bring food
      tonight in lieu of actual comedy material, did you?
      (*He reaches over with a napkin and dabs grease away from
      my mouth.*)
  Me: It's the sauce.
Dave: I know, the sauce. Put that down!
      (*I grudgingly put down the sandwich to tell a joke.*)
Dave: If this is real funny, maybe you'll get another
      sandwich.
  Me: Then I'll make it *extra funny*, Dave!

■　■　■

Merv Griffin started having me on his show in the late seventies and was always very supportive. In fact, his was the first show I ever guest-hosted, just before I started guest-hosting for Johnny in 1986. But I'll never forget what happened after my very first standup appearance on Merv's show. I was still a complete unknown and thrilled to have had another national television shot. A few days afterward, Merv's staff forwarded me a letter that they'd received: *My very first fan letter!* It was well written, perfectly formatted, cleanly typed, and wonderfully complimentary:

Dear Mr. Leno,
    I saw you on the *Merv Griffin Show*. He said it was one of your first times on TV. That's hard to believe, because you were so poised. I really enjoyed it. I'm sure you'll have a long future!
Yours truly, Julie Somebody

I couldn't have been more touched. So I sat down and wrote her back:

    Thank you very much. Yours is my first fan letter. I'll treasure this. Thank you for your kindness.
Your pal, Jay Leno

I put my home return address on it and sent it off. A few days later, I got another letter.

Dear Mr. Leno,
    I've never received such a prompt reply, especially a handwritten one from a celebrity. I'm very impressed. I'm a fan forever. Would you please send an autographed picture of yourself and I'll send you a picture of me.
Love, Julie

Again, this was very nice. So I sent off a signed eight-by-ten, once more thanking her for the kind words.

The next letter I received was completely different: It appeared to be written in crayon on a paper bag. I opened it and two Polaroids dropped out. At first, I couldn't quite figure out what I was looking at. Then I realized that they were close-up shots of a woman's torso, from her chest to her knees. The legs were spread apart and there appeared to be some sort of foreign object between them. I began to read the letter, which was full of obscenities and hard consonants: *suck this and stick that!* It was just vile.

And it was signed by the same woman!

I thought, "OH, GEEZ, I'M CORRESPONDING WITH A PSYCHO! AND SHE KNOWS WHERE I LIVE!"

That night, I went down to Canter's Deli, where all the comedians used to hang out, and I told the guys what had happened.

Tom Dreesen grinned and said, "Was her name Julie?"

"Yeah!"

"Oh, she writes every comic! Did you get two pictures?"

So much for early fan mail.

■ ■ ■

Toward the end of his great run as a talk show host, Merv Griffin taped his shows on a six-week delay. Of course, this made it difficult to keep a daily show current. And sometimes it made for surreal situations. Once, I was on the show with another guest who was a well-known television actor. A few weeks after we taped the show, he accidentally drowned in his swimming pool. But our show aired a couple of weeks after that. And there he was telling Merv, "I just put a pool behind my house. Boy, Merv, it's the best thing I ever did! I love that pool!"

The circumstance of my debut as a guest host was equally strange—and it proved to be another classic case of fate, not unlike what happened with *Dean Martin's Comedy World.* Naturally, I was very excited to host an actual talk show. This was a huge event in my life. Among the guests that day were three strippers who appeared in a documentary. (I'm not sure what it means that strippers seemed to figure in every stage of my career!) Before the show, one of them accidentally wandered into my dressing room, naked. I thought, "Well, a guy could get used to this guest-hosting thing!"

But then something terrible happened. Just prior to taping, I was in the greenroom with the guests, going over last-minute stuff. Suddenly, someone turned up the volume on a television monitor and people gathered around to watch the launch of the space shuttle *Challenger.* And, of course, within seconds, it had exploded. Everyone stood there stunned and crying. But, because the show wouldn't air for another six weeks, we went ahead and taped anyway. It was a little tricky to do comedy after such a tragic event. The audience was still in shock and not all that eager to laugh. But somehow I got through it okay.

And I couldn't help but think of Johnny Carson, who went on and did the monologue, night after night, year after year, no matter what had happened in the world that day, be it plane crashes or assassinations or war outbreaks. He would still be there, doing his job better than anyone else ever could. At that moment, I couldn't have appreciated him more.

In putting this book together, I was flipping through some of my early diary notebooks. (Most of the pages were blank, by the way. Keeping a diary just *seemed* like a good idea.) Anyway, on a page dated April 28, 1972, my twenty-second birthday, I found a short entry that I'd forgotten I ever made. All it said was: "Hope to host *The Tonight Show* someday. Maybe Johnny will leave."

Certainly, Johnny would leave on vacations. Maybe I could *guest-host*, anyway! Of course, all sorts of people had filled in for him over the years. Joan Rivers had become permanent guest host for a while, then she left to do her own show. So they started trying new people. Meanwhile, I hadn't done *The Tonight Show* in about six years. But I guess that Johnny's executive producers, Fred De Cordova and Peter Lassally, had been taking note of my Letterman appearances and thought that it was time for me to come back. So I did a few shots with Johnny that seemed to go very well. Finally, in late 1986, I was asked to be a regular guest host, alternating with Garry Shandling. Obviously, next to my very first shot in 1977, this was the greatest thrill of my entire career.

On that first day, I proudly pulled up to the NBC guard gate in Burbank. The guard looked at me blankly, as though he had no idea who I was.

"Yes?"

I said, "I'm Jay Leno."

"Where are you going?"

"*The Tonight Show.*"

"Uh, just a minute."

The guard picked up the phone, mumbled something about a "Jim Reynolds" into the receiver, then hung up.

Graduation day at school: the students and the teacher.

Jim Reynolds?

"Sorry, your name's not on the list."

I said, "I think you had the wrong name. It's Leno. Jay Leno."

The guard said, "What do you do?"

"I'm hosting the show tonight."

He looked at me very condescendingly and let out a long sigh.

"I hate to tell you this, son, but *Johnny Carson* is the host of *The Tonight Show!*"

"I know that! And I'm filling in!"

He shook his head and picked up the phone again.

Anyway, I guess I got in.

▪ ▪ ▪

This theme of general disbelief dogged me more often than I can say: Not long afterward, I had a gig in Columbus, Ohio, and was asked by the NBC affiliate station to do a live interview on the five-thirty news. I went over to the station at the appointed time and learned that the news anchorwoman would interview me after the next commercial break. The break came and I went over to introduce myself.

She said, "Hello. Look, you'll have to forgive me, but I'm not familiar with your work. This is kind of new to me. Can you quickly tell me a little about yourself?"

I said, "That's okay. I'm a comedian and I'm playing the Columbus Theatre. I also just started guest-hosting for Johnny Carson on *The Tonight Show*."

She jotted down some notes and said, "Oh, okay, thanks." I sat there until we came back from the commercial.

Then she turned to the camera and said, "I'm now talking with comedian Jay Leno. Jay, who *claims* to have hosted *The Tonight Show*—"

I cut in: "I'm not *claiming*! I have proof! I can prove it!"

Like I was trying to put one over on the city of Columbus!

■   ■   ■

At one point in the mid-eighties, I was the third most frequent flier in the United States, racking up over three million miles while out doing gigs. On one plane trip, I was seated on the aisle with two people next to me. The person next to the window leaned over and said, "Hey, you're Jay Leno! Would you mind signing an autograph for my mother?" No problem. Got her name and wrote her a little note. People were walking by, and about every third or fourth person nodded or smiled at me.

I signed my name a few more times. All very nice. At one point, the person sitting by the window got up to move around. All the while, the guy sitting next to me had been reading quietly. Finally, he cleared his throat and said, "You seem to be signing your name a lot. I guess I should know who you are."

I said, "Oh, no, not really. I'm just on TV."

"What do you do?"

"I fill in for Johnny Carson when he's not there. I guest-host on *The Tonight Show*."

He said, "I watch that show every night and I've never seen you there."

I said, "Well, I usually do it on Mondays when Johnny's not working."

"I've never seen you."

"Well, sir, I'm on!"

The sad part is that I had to have a flight attendant vouch for me. But I just attract a lot of odd people. Once I was sitting in an airport lounge across from a guy with a big smirk on his face. A couple of people walked over to say hello and ask for an autograph. Each time, the guy across from me smirked a little more. A couple of other people waved to me. The guy couldn't take it anymore.

He said, "Hey, I don't care who you are! What do you think of that, huh?"

I said, "That's fine. Hi, my name is Jay."

"I know *who* you are! I just don't care! And I don't want your autograph, okay? What do you think of that?"

"Well, that's fine."

"That pisses you off, doesn't it?"

I said, "No, it doesn't bother me, sir. It's fine! It's fine!"

241

"Well, I think it does!"

And then he proceeded to tell every person who passed by, *"Hey, he's pissed off because I don't want his autograph!"*

"I AM NOT PISSED OFF, OKAY?!"

■ ■ ■

The more people got used to me being on television, the more the press found new and different ways to describe me physically. This, I guess, is the price of renown, which isn't such a bad thing. I had understood *lantern-jaw* and *strong chin*. But I was amazed by what fodder my face was for further adjectival speculation. At one point, I even brought a stack of clippings onto *The Tonight Show* to share with Johnny. Some of my personal favorites:

> From *Cosmopolitan:* "Leno, *whose chin is the size of West Virginia* . . ."
>
> From the *Los Angeles Times:* "Leno, the *pelican-faced comedian* . . ."
>
> From the *Birmingham News:* "The *anvil-faced Leno* . . ."
>
> From *Seventeen:* "Leno *looks like a guy who got his start performing in the lounge of* Psycho's Bates Motel . . ."
>
> From the *Philadelphia Inquirer:* "Leno's blue eyes dart *like ferrets caged in a narrow face* . . ."
>
> From the *Washington Post:* "Leno might be intimidating if not for the *friendly, goofy look on his puss* . . ."
>
> And maybe the best, from *GQ:* "Leno, *whose head is ideal for a comedian, looks like a hunk of urban folk art* . . ."

Of course, I understand the urge to focus on my big countenance. Years earlier, when I'd been on television only a few times, I had a press agent who wanted to get me more atten-tion. So he hatched a scheme and created something he called the American Caricature Association. Then he wrote a press release announcing that I had been voted the Best Face to car-icature in the country. The item got picked up in papers every-where.

Jerry Seinfeld saw this and called me, all excited: "Man, that's great! I can't believe that they even know who you are!"

I said, "Jerry, I'm *president* of the American Caricature Association. We just made it up!"

He was furious: "You can't do that!"

It just drove him batty. So I voted him Best Face the next year.

■ ■ ■

I have a habit of always trying to reason with psychos and eccentric people. Maybe I'm being naive, but if you actually listen and talk to them, they calm down fairly quickly. Perhaps the weirdest example of this behavior happened just a couple of years ago—in my own home! Every night at around eleven-thirty, a few *Tonight Show* writers would come up to the house to work with me on the next day's monologue. They'd drive over, press the buzzer at the front gate, and I'd buzz them in. Then I'd usually leave the door to the house unlocked, so they could just walk right into the den. One night, I was sitting there watching the news, waiting for the guys to show up. The gate buzzed and I buzzed back. A few seconds later, an enor-mous man with wild eyes burst into the room!

He was out of breath and screaming my name. Which can get your attention right away. Also, he was waving a well-worn

Bible wrapped in rubberbands and dog-eared from constant reference. But no guns, knives, or bludgeoning instruments, at least.

I said, "Whoa! Calm down, calm down. Have a seat."

"Oh, Jay . . . you gotta help me . . ."

I said, "Did you come here to kill anybody or anything?"

He said, "No, no, I'm not gonna kill anybody. No, it's not that. See, I've got my Bible, right here . . ."

"All right, good. So what do you want?"

"You've gotta help me get in touch with Jerry Brown."

It was an election year, and since the former California governor was running for president, this guy was starting to rant about getting Jerry Brown's help for something.

I said, "Okay, take it easy."

Meanwhile, my second phone line rang.

I told him, "Hang on, hang on."

I picked up the phone. It was Mavis calling from upstairs.

"What's going on down there? Why is it so noisy?"

"Oh, it's just some psycho, honey. I'll talk to you later."

I turned back to the guy, who continued his raving. I said, "Look. Calm down, take it easy. I don't know Jerry Brown. If you call my office on Monday, let me see if I can get in touch with him. It's kind of late right now."

He began to compose himself.

"But I don't think I can wait that long . . ."

I said, "Well, I think Jerry Brown's campaign headquarters are down on Third Street. Maybe there's someone still there. Campaign people sometimes work through the night."

Very agreeably, he just said, "Okay."

Then he leaped off the chair and just ran out the door as

wildly as he'd come in. Meanwhile, Jimmy Brogan was just pulling up in his car to come work on the monologue. He walked in a few seconds later, looking concerned.

He said, "Some crazy guy just went flying out the front gate!"

"Oh, yeah, he was just here. You know, one of the usual psychos."

I started locking the door from that day on.

Another time, I was sleeping in the front of a plane. Suddenly, I was awakened by a man who said, "Mr. Leno, can you please just read this letter on *The Tonight Show*? Here's all the money I have! Please! Please!" He dumped a letter on my lap as well as one hundred eighty-five dollars—in singles and fives. Then he turned and ran back toward his seat in the rear. I didn't even get a look at him. I opened the letter, which seemed to be a legitimate plea to save the rain forests. But, of course, I couldn't read it on television. Comedians have no place on pulpits. And I certainly didn't want this guy's money.

But I didn't know who he was. So I had to get up and start wandering down the aisles of the plane to look for him. I stopped at every man and asked, "Excuse me, did you just give me one hundred eighty-five dollars?" And, one by one, they would say, "What? No, but will you sign this?" So now it looked like I was this show business jerk trying to meet everyone on the plane and fish for compliments! Finally, I found the guy and gave back the money. He said, "But that's all the money I have! I can get you more!" I said, "I don't want any more money!"

■ ■ ■

One of my strangest days in this peculiar realm took place in Washington, D.C., about six years ago. I was scheduled to speak at a Press Club luncheon, so I'd flown in very late the night before and checked into my hotel, around the corner from the White House. I got a few hours' sleep before the phone rang at about eight in the morning. I picked it up and heard an urgent Middle Eastern voice:

"Is theese Meester Leenos?"

"Uh, yes."

"My name ees Ahkmed Something-or-other, and I am calling you from somewhere in Virgeenia. I cannot tell you where!"

I said, "All right, fine. What's up?"

"I am calling on behalf of Meester Salman Rushdie! He weeshes to do your program."

At that point, Salman Rushdie had just gone into hiding, because the Ayatollah Khomeini put a price on his head for writing the novel *The Satanic Verses*.

I said, "Salman Rushdie wants to do *The Tonight Show?*"

"Yes, yes!"

"Well, I'm just a guest host. Johnny Carson is the host—"

"No, no. He wants to do the show weeth you!"

Great. Let the terrorists come kill Rushdie and me at the same time and we'll televise it. This smelled like a crackpot from top to bottom.

I said, "Well, all right. Have him call my office."

Years later, Rushdie did do the show with me—once we beefed up NBC security and put *two* guys out front.

Anyway, a few minutes after I hung up, the phone rang again. This voice was also all business, but American.

"President of the United States calling for Jay Leno."

Yeah, right. I wondered if a bulletin as to my whereabouts had gone out to every wacko in town.

I just rolled my eyes and said, "Great, great. Just put him through."

Short pause, then:

"Jay! George Bush."

For a second, I thought it was Dana Carvey. Because Bush sounds just like Carvey. In fact, Bush does the best Carvey around. But, impossible as it seemed, I quickly got the feeling that this was the real thing.

"Uh, President Bush, how are you, sir?"

"Fantastic! Say, what are you doing?"

"Gee, Mr. President, I just got in to do the Press Club luncheon."

"Well, we'd like to have you come over after the luncheon and say hello. Would you like to do that?"

I said, "Oh, that would be a great honor, Mr. President. But I have to fly out right after the luncheon. I'm sorry, I feel terrible."

He said, "Well, what are you doing right now?"

"Nothing."

Nothing but taking surreal phone calls, that is.

"Want to come over and have a glass of orange juice?"

"Sure, that would be a terrific honor."

"Listen, you're staying right across the street, so I'll have your name at the gate. Come on over!"

"Thank you, Mr. President. I'll be there in a few minutes."

There was only one problem. And, naturally, it was a ridiculous one. From Washington, I was scheduled to go directly to Massachusetts for a show. And I had arranged to meet an odd man there who'd agreed to sell me one of his antique motorcycles. He wanted eighteen thousand dollars for it, but would take only cash. So, before leaving Los Angeles, I got the money and stuffed it in my carry-on bag. But now I didn't want to leave the money in my hotel room while I walked over to the White House. So I called down to the front desk and said, "Do you have any duct tape? I've got a broken suitcase."

They sent up a roll right away. Then I proceeded to take the eighteen thousand in five-hundred-dollar packets and tape all of the money to my chest. I put on my shirt, my tie, and my suit coat, and checked myself in the mirror. There was no bulking. You could never tell. Perfect. So I walked over to the White House and stopped at the guard gate.

I said, "Jay Leno to see the President." Which was a great deal of fun to say.

They sent me through an X-ray detector.

No problem. I was told to go right down the driveway to the house itself. I got there, and another guard led me to a second X-ray machine.

I said, "I just went through the X-ray at the gate . . ."

"You have to go through again, sir."

Apparently, this machine was more sensitive than the first. Because the guard said, "What do you have under your shirt?"

Oh, no.

I said, "Well, um, I . . ."

"Could you open your shirt for me, please?"

I started unbuttoning and explained like an idiot, "Well, there's this guy in Massachusetts and I'm buying this motorcy-

Here I am, hoping that I won't be strip-searched by Marlin Fitzwater.

cle from him later and he wanted eighteen grand, but only in cash . . ."

The guard saw the money taped all over my chest and, suddenly, his face reddened with embarrassment. He must have thought I was transporting some Iran-Contra hush money to the Oval Office! And he obviously didn't want to be in possession of that kind of information.

He said, "Go ahead, please!"

"No, no. Don't misunderstand. It's not for the President. This is for a motor—"

"Please! Go ahead! Go ahead!"

"It's for a motorcycle I'm buying later . . ."

"Fine, fine. Just go ahead, please!"

So I went in and met the President in my Eighteen-Thousand-Dollar Suit. We had a very pleasant chat, considering whatever monologue jokes I may have made at his expense. Not the least of which dealt with his chief of staff, John Sununu, who'd been caught using government planes for personal travel. (One joke that I'd been doing: "The President is jogging a lot these days. But I guess he has no other way to get around. Sununu took the limo!")

So it was only inevitable that the President said to me, "Jay, I've got a big fan of yours here! You know John Sununu, don't you?"

"Oh, uh, sure!"

Sununu came in and he was just *thrilled* to meet me. He looked down at the carpet and kind of grumbled, "Oh, hello."

Then I took a little tour of the White House before it was time to leave. On my way out, I saw the guard again.

I said to him, "Thanks again. By the way, I still have the money right here—"

And I began to unbutton my shirt again to show him.

He just looked the other way and waved me on by, blurting out, "Thank you! Goodbye, sir! Goodbye now!"

"But I—"

"*Goodbye, sir!*"

■ ■ ■

One Sunday afternoon, Mavis and I were tooling around in my big '57 Buick Roadmaster convertible, and we decided to head down to Hard Times Pizza on Santa Monica Boulevard in West Hollywood. We edged toward the area and found traffic at a standstill. People were lining the street and others were marching down Santa Monica. We suddenly realized that it was the annual Gay Pride Parade. Then I saw a cop waving me through the blockade. He was tooting his whistle and hollering, "Come this way!"

I said to Mavis, "You see that, honey? The cop recognizes me from TV!"

I'm not a big one for taking special privileges, but I figured if being a big shot meant that I could cut through the line to get my pizza—fine with me!

The cop sent us out onto Santa Monica and positioned us behind a couple of guys in a '57 Chevy. At which point, it occurred to me: "Oh, geez, that cop didn't recognize me! He just thinks we're part of the parade!"

Suddenly, people who were watching from the sidewalk began pointing at us.

And I heard them saying: "Hey, look at that! I didn't know Leno was gay!"

"I'M JUST GOING FOR A SLICE OF PIZZA!"

But they were waving and hooting!

"Right on, Jay!"

Mavis was cracking up. So I turned to her and said, "Go ahead and laugh! They think you're a lesbian!"

We were stuck in the parade for the next four miles.

People kept waving and we waved back, all the while listening to hundreds of gay people holler:

"Hey, Jay's gay!"

And: "Jay, thank you for coming out! Thank you for being so strong!"

"I'M NOT REALLY COMING OUT! I JUST WANTED SOME PIZZA!"

I guess doors open when you get famous. But I never figured that *that* door would be one of them.

▪ ▪ ▪

Back in the very early eighties before people really knew of me, Gene Braunstein and I were riding motorcycles way up on Mulholland Drive, which snakes above the Hollywood Hills all the way out toward the ocean. We pulled off onto a broken-up old road that perched above a small enclave of houses and, just beyond that, the sweeping vista of the San Fernando Valley. We climbed off our bikes and stood there looking out at the view. A few minutes later, a BMW drove up, and a man and a woman got out. I figured they had come to take in the view as well. They quietly walked up behind us. Then the man pulled out a .38 revolver and stuck the nuzzle against the back of my head.

He screamed, "Hold it right there! Hold it right there!"

I said, "Hey, hey! What's this all about?"

"I saw you guys from my house down below! You're the bikers who robbed my house!"

"We didn't rob your house!"

The woman, who must have been his wife, said, "Honey, take it easy!"

He said, "No! I finally got these sons of bitches! I knew you'd come back!"

"We didn't come back! We're just looking at the valley! Honest!"

"Don't lie to me!"

Then he cocked the gun!

I said, "Look, just take it easy. It wasn't us! I'm an entertainer . . . Here's my license and ID." I carefully pulled out my wallet and handed him some cards.

The wife said, "Oh, maybe it's not them, honey."

"Sure, it's them! Why else would they be standing here looking down at our house?"

I said, "Gee, I've never robbed anybody. You can check. I've been on *The Tonight Show* a couple of times!"

He said, "Well, I've never heard of you! I don't know who you are!"

I said, "Look, I don't have any weapons or anything. This is my friend Gene Braunstein. He's from Connecticut. I'm from Massachusetts."

Finally, the guy calmed himself and wrote down my name and license number. Then he said, "All right. Just get the hell outta here! And never come back!"

No problem. We got back on our bikes and peeled off.

About seven years later, after I'd moved to Beverly Hills, I drove over to do some grocery shopping at a little store on Beverly Glen, off Mulholland. As I wandered through the aisles, a voice behind me said, "Jay Leno?"

I turned around and saw a man with a big grin on his face. He said, "Remember me?"

"Um, gosh, no. Sorry."

He said, "I'm the guy who pulled the gun on you! Remember? I thought you robbed my house?"

It was him!

"Oh, how are you? I didn't recognize you without the gun . . ."

He slapped me on the back and said, "Oh, man, I've been following your career. You're doing great! I'm so happy for you!

And my kid is your biggest fan! He loves you! Say, could you sign an autograph for him?"

Only in Los Angeles.

"Sure, sure."

"Oh, thanks, you're the best!"

I wrote: "To Michael, Your dad's got a great gun. Best, Jay Leno."

15

FIGHT
THE GOOD FIGHT

I always told my dad that if I ever made it in show business, I'd buy him a Cadillac and a Lincoln. So, as soon as I started guest-hosting for Johnny, I went back to Andover and took him shopping for a Cadillac. (The Lincoln would come later.) Cadillac salesmen are different from any other car salesmen, especially back East. They demonstrate affluence by wearing loud plaid jackets and smoking big cigars. Which is to say, their taste sometimes just seemed questionable. And, on that day, the salesman led my father directly to a white '86 Caddy with a red velour interior.

My dad wanted it on sight.

The salesman said, "Now, Mr. Leeno, your Cadillac can have a regular interior . . . or you can have what you're looking at now—this, the beeyooteeful interior *dee elee-gaance!*"

Of course, the "interior de elegance" was just the worst of Detroit—big, tufted, rolled upholstery. It looked like it belonged in Elvis's coffin. When you sat on it, you'd sink three feet into

Taken on the day Mavis and I got married. Mom is thinking, "Finally, I can rest."

the down cushion. After twenty minutes, your back would be killing you. But, for the first thirty seconds, it felt like a feather bed.

Naturally, my father's eyes lit up. "Hey, I like the sound of that! Interior dee elee-gaance!"

So that's what we got. Then we drove it home to show my mom, who hated the idea of a Cadillac to begin with. In fact, she deplored ostentatiousness of any kind. She would say, "We're not Cadillac people! We're simple people!"

She came out to meet us in the driveway and covered her eyes with shame. Especially when she saw the red velour. To her, this looked like a brothel on wheels. From that day forward, when they rode around in the Cadillac, she would slump down below window level so people wouldn't see her. And she'd mutter, "We look like *Who's Who* driving down the street in this thing! *We're not Cadillac people!*"

My father, on the other hand, would honk at everyone in town and holler, "HEY, MY BOY BOUGHT THIS FOR ME!"

Which, of course, was the basic difference between my parents. When my father came to see my shows, his greatest thrill was to stand up and wave to the crowd: "HEY, THAT'S MY BOY UP ON THE STAGE!" He enjoyed nothing more than giving out my home phone number to people he met on the street who were fans of mine: "Call him up! He'd love to hear from you!" Whenever he heard somebody on television tell a joke that he liked, he'd call and tell me to use it. I'd say, "Dad, I can't! It's Jerry Seinfeld's joke!" And he'd say, "Oh, just go ahead! He won't mind."

Show business almost seemed to suit him better than it did me. One day, he went outside to get the paper at the end of the driveway. He found a guy there who'd been waiting for hours to meet him. The guy said, "Oh, hello, Mr. Leno. I'm a magician and I'd like to get in touch with your son . . ."

My father said, "A magician, huh? Let's see your act!" He stood out there for the next forty-five minutes, happily watching a magic show on the lawn. Then he gave the magician my home phone number: "Call him up! He'll put you on that *Tonight Show*, no problem!"

▪ ▪ ▪

In 1986, I played Carnegie Hall, which my parents wouldn't have missed for the world. And they brought every relative in the tri-state area. I had been to Carnegie Hall only once before—when I crawled through a window one day in the early seventies and sneaked onto the empty stage. I had wondered what it would feel like to work there. Then somebody yelled, "Hey, what are you doing?" And I ran for my life.

This time I hoped to last a little longer onstage. Certainly, I wanted to do right by my folks. To class things up a bit, I'd hired a little three-piece string ensemble to play before I started my act. And this immediately impressed my mother. Usually, she would come to shows with a somewhat pained expression on her face, never quite understanding what was going on. But, seeing the musicians as she walked in, she said, "Oh, now I like that! Much better than always with the jokes!"

The ushers took them to their seats, fifth row center, along with Mavis and all the relatives. Which I guess turned into some kind of minor production of its own. Three nineteen-year-old boys sitting directly behind them must have quickly figured out that these were my parents. One of the kids leaned forward, tapped my dad's shoulder, and asked, "You're Jay's father, aren't you?"

My father, for all his showbiz enthusiasm, never actually got used to the idea that I had somehow become famous. And he never fully understood that I'd aged beyond my teen years. So he sprightfully turned to the kids behind him and said, "Hey, you know my boy? Have you been over to our house?"

He figured that these must have been some of the kids I worked with at McDonald's!

"Uh, no, we're just fans."

If that confused them, there was more to come.

I finally took the stage, and the crowd couldn't have been

more receptive. I started doing my material, some of which the kids behind my parents must have known from watching me on the Letterman show. They were laughing at the setups *and* the payoffs. My mother, of course, didn't know what to make of such eager laughter. So, at one point, she turned around, pressed a finger to her lips, and went, *"Sshhhhhhh! Sssshhhhhhh! Quiet!"*

I saw this from the stage. And I just stopped the show.

"Ma! Don't shush people! It's a comedy show! They're sup-posed to be laughing!"

This mortified her! To be singled out in public was the worst of all embarrassments imaginable. And at Carnegie Hall yet!

But she knew that this was one of my favorite things to do to her. And so I did it whenever possible. Once, she and my Aunt Faye came to Atlantic City to see me perform. But, that night, when I stepped onstage, their front-row seats were empty. So I said to the audience, "Where's Mom? Oh, here she comes!" That was horrifying enough to rattle her completely. The two of them had been out in the casino playing the slot machines. And now, feeling everyone's eyes upon them, they crept self-consciously toward their table, holding plastic con-tainers full of nickels. Just as they got down front, my mother nervously dropped all her nickels on the floor.

CRRAAAAASSSSHHHH!

Which gave me another opportunity to tease her.

"Maaaaaaa! Can you hold it down! I'm trying to work up here!"

Absolute humiliation. I even took this exercise into the private sector. As a kid and all the way into adulthood, I would take her to supermarkets, then sneak off to have her paged over the intercom. I'd tell the store manager, "I'm trying to find my mother. She's an elderly woman and she tends to forget where she is. I'm sure she thinks that she's lost."

She'd be off picking produce when the PA system would ring out with:

"We're paging a Mrs. Leno! If you are lost, Mrs. Leno, please meet your son at the manager's office!"

Like a sprinter, she would come tearing through the store to find me and scream, "Ohhh! Would you stop doing that! Stop doing that! Don't ever do that!"

■　■　■

Of course, my mom could dish it out as well as take it. For instance, she elevated the art of backseat driving to new peaks of annoyance. She had an ability to never actually state her complaints aloud. Instead, she would sing them in a shrill little voice, then pretend that she hadn't said anything—just to make you crazy. It happened whenever she and my father came out to visit me in Los Angeles. I'd drive them around and point out various sites.

"Mom, this is Jimmy Stewart's house."

"Oh, we could enjoyyyyy the house if we weren't speeding byyy-yiiii it . . ."

"What's that, Mom?"

"Nothing, nothing."

I'd drive along for a while.

"There's a stop siii-iignnn . . ."

"I saw the sign, Mother."

"I said nothing!"

Then: "*But we'd enjoyyy oursellvvves if we weren't speee-eeeding . . .*"

She also had a habit of giving automotive advice when she had no idea what she was talking about. One day I had her in the car when I got a flat tire. I opened the trunk to get a jack, but it wasn't there. I came back and told her, "Mom, we got a flat, there's no jack. So I can't change the tire. We've gotta wait for the tow truck."

"Well, did you check the battery?"

"Ma, it's got nothing to do with the battery! It's a flat tire, which I can't change without a jack—"

"Your father always checks the battery whenever there's a problem with the car."

I rolled my eyes and figured there was no point arguing with her.

"All right, you want me to check the battery? I'll check the battery."

So I opened the hood and said, "Mom, I checked the battery, it's not the battery. The battery is fine!"

"Well, now we know for sure."

■ ■ ■

One thing she would never tolerate was anyone who took the Lord's name in vain. Me, especially. This was a huge issue with her. She would say, "People might steal money because they have to eat. Or maybe they get into a fight to protect somebody, then they go to prison. But there's no reason to ever take the Lord's name in vain!"

I remember being home in the mid-eighties, watching the Roberto Duran–Sugar Ray Leonard fight on TV with my dad.

He always liked having someone see the fights with him. So we were caught up in the action. Punches flew back and forth. Then one of the fighters took a fall. And I hollered, "Oh, *Christ*! He barely got hit! Look at that!"

Then I heard what I thought sounded like hoofbeats approaching: *thump thump thump thump*. The whole house was rattling.

I wondered, "What's that? An earthquake?"

Then suddenly: BONNNK!

My mother hit me on the head with a pot. The last time that happened was when I got caught ditching high school!

"*Owwwwww!*"

"Not in this house!"

I saw birds. "Whaaaaaa . . . ?"

"You'll not say that in this house!"

I felt a dent in the side of my head!

My father looked over and shrugged: "Oh, gee, that's right, son. Don't say that in front of your mother!"

"*I forgot!*"

■ ■ ■

There was never a moment when my parents actually discouraged me from going into show business. Early on, my Aunt Nettie would tell my mom, "Ooooooh, he's *weeeestin'* his time! He's not goooonna meeeke it in show business! Look at young Bobby Peterson—now *he's* got himself a good job down at the factory!" And, truth be told, my mother probably would have liked to see me in a steadier line of work. Especially during my first years in Los Angeles, which seemed to her like I had gone off to seek my fortune as a panhandler in a foreign nation. At the time, I would always exaggerate the accomplishments of other people in show business, hoping that she would better understand the possibilities that lay before me.

For instance, Sylvester Stallone had just signed an enormous deal to make the movie *F.I.S.T.* So I called home and said, "You know, Ma, Stallone just got twelve million dollars for ten weeks' work!"

And she actually said, "Yeah? But then what happens those other forty-two weeks? What is he going to do if nothing else comes in? Then he's going to be stuck, isn't he?"

To my mom, it was always better to have a hundred and fifty bucks coming in every week than to get twelve million in cash up front. And even when I started making better than decent dough, she never quite comprehended it. Worse yet was the idea that I could spend it on her. This was inconceivable. Plus, she would never, ever ask for anything. During one of my trips home, I was sitting up with her at the kitchen table one night. She seemed a little out of sorts, so I asked her what was up.

She said, "You know, your father and I were at the mall today and I saw this blouse that I liked and it cost ninety dollars, but that's just too much money. Ah, well . . ."

I said, "You want the blouse? Here's a hundred dollars, go buy the blouse . . ."

And I pulled out the cash.

She said, "Oh, I can't take money from you. Your father would be so upset."

"Just take the hundred."

"Oh, no. If your father finds out . . ."

"He's not going to find out! Take the hundred bucks. Just don't tell Dad."

A small covert action like this represented the height of dishonesty to my mother.

"Well, I don't know. Maybe, if you think so . . ."

The next morning, I was sitting at breakfast with my dad, who said, "What the hell's wrong with your mother? She's all upset! She was up pacing the floor all night."

Oh, geez.

I said, "Gosh, I don't know."

My mother came into the kitchen, looking nervous. She started to pour my father's coffee.

He said, "So what do you gotta do today, honey? Going to do some shopping?"

"*Ahhhhhhh!*"

She leaped into the air and spilled coffee everywhere. Like she'd been caught pulling a Brink's job. I just went out and bought the blouse for her.

In my ongoing effort to bring my parents into the twentieth century—and against all their protestations—I once got them a VCR. I explained that they could now just tape *Matlock*—and watch it whenever they wanted! Which sounded like a dream come true! Plus, they could rent movies or look at tapes of my late-night TV appearances without having to stay up. But the problem was trying to explain how it worked. When it came to technology, my mother didn't even *want* to learn. You'd start talking about the automatic timer and her eyes would just glaze over. And when my father couldn't get the VCR to work, he just pulled out his screwdriver!

"Let me open up the back and take a look in there!"

I said, "Don't open the back, Dad!"

"Maybe there's a screw loose!"

"There's no screws in it, Dad. I'll program the clock on it for you. The rest is easy! You just press the button for what day you want to set for taping."

I turned to my mom and asked, "Now what day do you want to watch it?"

"I want to watch it today."

"It doesn't say 'today' on the machine, Ma! You have to press Wednesday."

"How does it know today is Wednesday?"

"It's got a brain, Mom! It just knows!"

When I told my mother you could tape one show while watching another show, you would have thought I'd said, "Men from Mars have landed! It's the end of the world! Advanced technology can go no further!"

None of it mattered, of course. Over the next several months, my phone bill showed hundreds and hundreds of dollars spent calling them to try to explain how to use this stupid videotape machine.

"LISTEN, MOM, TELL DADDY TO PUT THE TAPE IN AND PRESS PLAY! YOU HAVE TO PRESS PLAY!"

"Your father says it'll cause a fire!"

"*It's not gonna cause a fire! Press play!*"

"He's afraid to touch it!"

"*He survived the Depression! How could he be afraid to touch it?*"

And this whole nightmare started because I told a lie. When I told them I was getting them this videotape recorder, my mother said, "Those things cost hundreds of dollars! Your father and I don't want you spending all your money on a big gift!"

Like I had been in show business fifteen years and had only accumulated $379.95!

I said, "Mom, it's no big deal."

"It's too much money! We'll send it right back! Right back! We're not accepting it!"

So I lied: "Look, Ma, a friend of mine runs a video shop and he's giving me the wholesale price—twenty-five dollars!"

Pause.

"Well, twenty-five dollars isn't bad. Okay, you can spend twenty-five dollars. That's a fair amount."

Two weeks later, she sent me a check for a hundred dollars. She wanted four more machines for the neighbors.

▪ ▪ ▪

For the longest time, most of my relatives managed to function without the benefit of basic modern technology. My Aunt Edie, for instance, never got rid of her dial phones. Whenever I went to visit her with my parents, I couldn't make any long-distance calls, because access codes require punching the touch-tone numbers. So if I had to urgently get ahold of someone, I'd tell my mother that I needed to go find a pay phone. Which she never understood: "Oh, Mr. Big Shot! Mr. Fill-In for Johnny Carson! He's too important to use his aunt's dial phone!"

I remember the time in the late eighties when my Uncle Mike and Aunt Rose, then in their seventies, planned to visit my Uncle John, who lived in San Diego. I told Uncle Mike, "When you get to San Diego, call me in L.A. I won't be there, but leave a message on my machine and tell me where you'll be."

To avoid confusion, I made sure that my answering

machine had a very basic greeting: "Hi, this is Jay. I'm not in right now. Please leave your name and number."

So I got home from the road that particular Sunday and played my messages. And I heard:

"HELLLO? JAAAAAY? HELLLOOOOO? JAAAAAY, IT'S YOUR UNCLE MIKE!"

Then I heard him say to my Aunt Rose, "I don't know where he is! He picked up the phone, then he walked away!"

Then I heard my Aunt Rose say, "Well, maybe he's in the bathroom."

For the next ten minutes, I heard a television in the background. Like they were waiting for me to come out of the bathroom! Then finally he shouted, "JAAAAAY, JAAAAAY? I DON'T KNOW WHERE HE IS!" And he hung up.

Then he called my mom to tell her that I'd hung up on him!

She called me, furious, and said, "Why did you hang up on your Uncle Mike? He said he called you yesterday afternoon, you picked up the phone, you said hello, then you made a funny noise, and you hung up on them!"

"*I didn't hang up! I wasn't even home at the time! My machine picked up!*"

"Oh, Mr. Big Shot with a machine! Mr. Fancy had the machine answer the phone!"

"I'm not Mr. Fancy! Everybody has an answering machine!"

"Well, your father and I don't have a machine!"

"YOU'RE EIGHTY! YOU DON'T NEED AN ANSWERING MACHINE! NOBODY CALLS YOU!"

■ ■ ■

My father loved factory warranties. For every product he ever bought, he would fill out the warranty card and make a copy— "for our files." Just in case. One classic example: Back when I was a high school senior, he grabbed me one day as I walked into the house and said, "Come on, son. Let's go up to the hardware store. I want to get a new toilet seat for the bathroom." This was my father's idea of a great father-and-son outing. So I went with him. He walked into the store and told the clerk, "I want your best toilet seat! What do you recommend?"

After recovering from this request, the guy sold us an American Standard toilet seat—which my father especially liked because it came with a twenty-year guarantee.

Then, in 1988, I happened to be home again. I went in to use the john, sat down, and—*craaack!* The seat broke off at the hinge. I looked at it and saw it was rusty and rotted back there. I snapped it off and went to throw it away. I told my dad that I would run out and buy another one.

He said, "Wait a minute! Don't throw that away! I've got a twenty-year guarantee on that thing!"

It was the same seat! Within minutes, he pulled out the warranty—which at this point was a yellowed piece of paper that looked like the Magna Carta.

I said, "Put that away, Dad! I am not walking down Main Street with this rotted-out toilet seat!"

"Then I'll do it! I've got a guarantee!"

So I drove him over to the hardware store with this awful old seat and we walked in. People in the aisles were leaping out of our way. My father asked for the guy who sold us the seat. We found out that he had retired ten years earlier. But his son, who was like fifty-seven, came out.

Dad said, "MY TOILET SEAT BROKE. I WANT A NEW ONE."

The guy looked at it and said, "It's rotted! I can't give you a new one."

So my dad presented him with the warranty.

"OH YEAH? LOOK AT THIS! NINETY-TWO DAYS LEFT ON THE WARRANTY!"

The guy gave us a new seat. The warranty on that toilet seat promised to last until the year 2008. When we got home, he filled out the card and made a big show of putting it in my name. This was my inheritance!

■　■　■

Some men know how to retire. They have hobbies, they relax, they travel. My father was not one of those men. He hated to be unproductive. After he finally left the insurance business, he drove my mother nuts by wanting to add rooms onto the house. My mom would try to tell him, "No one lives here anymore! We don't need a rumpus room. I don't need a billiard room. We don't play billiards!"

For a while, he took up fishing with my Uncle Lou. But, as with any chore, he even had to do that to maximum effect. They'd bring home piles of fish and pack them into every freezer they could find. And, usually, that's where most of the fish stayed. One time when he and Lou were on their boat, they got lost in a thick fog. Both of them wore hearing aids and tended to let their batteries run down. The Coast Guard patrol found them floating in Boston Harbor only because they were screaming at each other.

"WHERE THE HELL ARE WE?"

"WHAT'S THAT?"

"I SAID WHERE THE HELL ARE WE?"

"YOU SAY WE'RE FAR? FAR FROM WHAT?"

I think all of New England heard them out there. But, hearing problems aside, my dad was generally always a fairly healthy specimen, hale and hearty. In the early eighties, there had been a flare-up of prostate trouble, but it seemed to disappear. I would call home every day to check up on both him and Mom. Then, at one point in 1990, I got my mother on the phone. One thing I knew about my mother was that she was the worst liar. I could always tell when she was trying to fudge the truth.

I said, "Hi, Mom, how you doing?"

"Oh, fine, everything's fine. Nothing to worry about."

"Gee, you sound like something's wrong."

"Oh, no, nothing's wrong, nothing at all. . . . Your father's going to be fine. . . ."

"Wait a minute! What do you mean 'going to be'? What happened?"

"Oh, gee, I'm not supposed to say . . ."

"Say what? Tell me."

"Oh, your father had to go in for another prostate operation. But it's nothing serious! The operation went well and he'll just be in the hospital for a couple of days. . . . But he knew that if I told you you'd come running home, so you're not supposed to know."

"Okay, Ma, I don't know anything about it."

We got off the phone and I immediately called the airlines. Like everyone else, I never liked to think about my parents in terms of mortality. But I wasn't about to ignore it, either. Plus, as long as I found out that the operation had been successful, the very least I could do was try to cheer my dad up a bit. So, without telling them, I got on a red-eye flight that night and arrived in Boston by six-thirty the next morning. I went directly to the hospital and found his doctor, who assured me that all was well. Then I asked a nurse to help me play a little joke. I wanted to surprise him somehow. So I had her get me a doctor's outfit—the full hospital greens with the cap and mask, as well as eyeglasses, a clipboard, and a stethoscope. I disguised myself completely, then walked into my father's room.

He looked up from his bed and, alert as ever, said, "Hey, hiya, Doctor! How are ya?"

I decided to take a stern, dismissive tone with him. "Fine, fine."

He didn't like the sound of me.

"Everything all right, Doctor?"

"Didn't I just tell you that everything's fine?"

"You seem a little upset there."

"Oh, no," I said. "But I was just looking at your chart here. Tsk, tsk. We get a lot of guys like you in here!"

"What are you talkin' about?"

"You know. Guys like you who come in here for a simple procedure, then stay a goddamn week trying to get a free meal and make other people pay for it!"

His eyes started to bulge with rage.

"WHAT? WHO THE HELL DO YOU THINK YOU'RE TALKIN' TO HERE?!"

"I'm talking to you—you goddamn lazy bum!"

With that, he leaped out of bed and started choking me. Then I saw he was about to punch me in the face!

So I yanked off the green mask and said, "Hey, Pop! It's me!"

He let go, stunned.

"Well, goddamnit! What the hell are you comin' in here like that? I coulda killed you!"

"I came here to play a trick on you!"

Once he calmed down, he thought that that was the funniest thing. Of course, I had gone for his Achilles' heel. The same way my mother was loath to be embarrassed in public, he couldn't bear the idea that anyone ever thought of him as a man of leisure. Much less a deadbeat or a burden. I was just lucky that I didn't end up in traction that day. But it was good to see that he had all of his vital signs.

■ ■ ■

The hardest thing for most families to do is to express affection for each other. And I guess nothing is harder for fathers and sons than expressing emotion. My dad and I were always real close. But sometime in my thirties I realized that I had never officially told my dad that I loved him. Of course, he knew that I loved him. And I knew that he loved me. But all guys aren't as good at this stuff as Phil Donahue and Alan Alda. It's so awkward. Mothers and daughters seem to have no problem with it. But fathers and sons do. That's just the way it is.

So, one year, I decided that I would call him on his birthday and tell him that I loved him. Make it official. Of course, the only thing more awkward than saying it in person is saying it on the telephone. But my mind was made up. On that day I called and he picked up in the same way he answered the phone all of his life.

"YALLLLLO!!! YALLLLLO DERE!"

"Hi, Dad! Happy Birthday!"

"WHO'S THIS?"

Who's this!

I said, "It's me, Dad!"

"OH, HALLO, SON!"

I sucked up the nerve and started, "Listen, you've been a pretty good dad and everything. So I just thought I'd call and let ya know that I, uh, that I, uh . . ." And here I just mumbled: ". . . *kinda-likeya-and-that-kindastuff* . . ."

"WHAT'S THAT? I CAN'T HEAR YA!"

Oh, boy. I tried again. "Oh, nothin', nothin'. It's just that I've been thinking about ya. You've been a good dad, you know, and I just wanted to letcha know that I, uh, you know, *careaboutchayouknow* . . ."

"WHAT'S THAT? ARE YA STUCK IN THE CAR? I CAN COME AND GET YOU."

"I'm not stuck! I'm fine! But I was thinkin' about ya. You've been a good dad, you know. God forbid something should happen, you know. I just wanted to let you know that, uh, that *I love ya! I wanted to let you know that I love ya, that's all!*"

"OH, YA LOVE ME! OKAY, I'M GONNA PUT YOUR MOTHER ON THE LINE NOW!"

"Okay, Pop, glad we had a chance to talk!"

■　■　■

My parents were with me through every high and low in my life, always supportive and proud of my accomplishments. Of course, there may not have been a prouder moment than when

I became Johnny Carson's successor as host of *The Tonight Show* on May 25, 1992. And I was especially proud to have made them so proud. Not that my mother didn't have enough trouble comprehending the national impact of even that particular triumph.

Two months before I was to debut, my face (as caricatured by Al Hirshfeld) appeared on the cover of *Time*. So I called her with the big news.

"Mom, I'm going to be on the cover of *Time* this week, so tell Daddy to pick up a bunch of copies."

"Oh, good. Now which one is it? Time what?"

"*Time* magazine, Mom!"

"I don't think we get that one around here."

"Mom, it's *Time* magazine! You get it! It's a very important magazine. And you should call Aunt Edie in New York and Aunt Faye in New Jersey and Uncle Louie in Florida and tell them, too."

"Oh, I don't think you'll be on the cover in *those places*. I mean, people know you're from the Boston area, so they put you on the cover of the magazine in this area!"

"Ma, I'm not only on the Andover edition! It's *Time* magazine! It goes all over the world!"

"I don't think so. . . ."

■　■　■

I always thought that my mom could have been the next Gracie Allen if she hadn't been so shy. As I said on *The Tonight Show*, just after she passed away, of all the comedians that I count as friends, none of them could make me laugh the way she did. She was simply the best friend I ever had. The same year that I took over *The Tonight Show*, she was diagnosed with lung cancer, and although she had beaten breast cancer before, she lived only another year. During that time there was the big media squall about whether I would keep my job. Thankfully, fate somehow prevailed in fairly short order. Because, aside from some of the comedy-club horror stories I've already relayed here, I've never been fired from a job in my life. That was something I never needed my parents to see. Even as a kid when I lost my job at Wilmington Ford, I got it back before they ever knew.

And all through that same time my dad would get worked up as only he could. If there was ever a bad review in the paper, he'd say, "I'm gonna get that fella on the phone!" It was no different than when he found out that I was actually working at The Improv *for free*! And, just as I did back then, I told him, "Dad, don't call the man! Everyone is entitled to their own opinions." But he never stopped telling me, "Hey, you just get in there and fight the good fight, son!" And so I did. As well as I could.

But after Mom died on June 26, 1993, he sort of lost his own will to fight. After fifty-seven years of marriage, he went downhill pretty fast. Prostate cancer caught up with him and he passed away on August 17 the following year.

But none of this is meant to be maudlin. Because I never think of them as gone. I've got all of their stories and that keeps them nearby always. When my mother's health was failing, she actually used to worry about what I would do for material without her around. But she's always around, always not quite getting it, always being funnier than she pretended to be.

Anyway, besides all of the goofy stuff I've already told you, here's one last story that ought to give you a good idea of exactly what kind of parents they were:

When I was only fourteen, before I had my driver's license, I scraped up three hundred fifty bucks to buy a crappy old '34 Ford pickup truck. Even though I couldn't legally drive it, I just wanted to have my own car. The truck actually ran, but it was a dented-up nightmare. Every day after school I worked on fixing it up—sanding, filing, painting, buffing. As a present, my mom and dad got me brand-new Naugahyde upholstery for the seats. Then, one day, I slammed a door a little too hard and the window just shattered. I didn't have any money to replace it.

Around that same time I finally got my driver's license. My favorite thing to do was to drive myself to school. Andover High was a big flat building, where you could see the parking lot from every classroom. One day it began to rain hard. Because of the broken glass, I sat in class and watched my truck—and the new upholstery—get thoroughly drenched. And I couldn't do a thing about it.

Then, suddenly, through the window, I saw my mom and dad tear into the parking lot. They screeched up next to my truck and dragged a huge piece of plastic out of their car. Then they covered the truck in the pouring rain. My dad had known that the rain would ruin the upholstery. So he left the office in the middle of the day, picked up my mom, and bought this hunk of plastic to save my seats.

I watched them do this. And I just began crying right there in class. That memory has always stayed with me.

There are so many things to miss about them. But one thing I especially miss is calling home after each *Tonight Show* taping just to explain to my mother who the guests were: "*His name is Tom Cruise, Ma! Yes, he's a big star. Trust me!*"

ACKNOWLEDGMENTS

Up until now there was only one author in my house and she knows more about books than I ever hoped to. For a long time, my wife, Mavis, told me that she thought all of the dopey stories that I've always loved recounting would make for a funny collection of memoirs. Without her vision—and her keen editorial eye during the process of making it a reality—this book might not have existed.

Expressing myself has always been my one proven skill, but finding my voice on the page was going to be a different challenge. Fortunately, my old friend Bill Zehme, senior writer at *Esquire* magazine, was with me to help make that transition practically effortless. I think I started telling him stories fourteen years ago, and in the course of doing many magazine pieces together, he was able to remind me of things I'd almost forgotten and then shape and structure them into the form you now see.

I owe special thanks to my brother, Pat, who refreshed old memories and dug up embarrassing pictures—and, most important, helped take such good care of our parents when they were ill. Knowing that he was just down the street from them—and always there—made my job of telling jokes on television a lot easier during that difficult time.

Meanwhile, back in Burbank and Big Dog Productions, Helga Pollock stayed the course and oversaw every imaginable detail involved in making this project happen. And thanks as well to Justine Bartoli, who aided and abetted Helga throughout the process. Other people who made great contributions for which I am grateful are Mauro DiPreta, my editor, a nice Italian boy of indefatigable spirit; Alan Berger, Jeff Berg, and Amanda Urban at ICM; Jimmy Brogan, who knows when a story and a joke work; Lennie Sogoloff, who gave me my start at his club, Lennie's on the Turnpike, and took time to compose his own memories of those crazy days; Gene Braunstein, who remembers it all too well; John Miller and John Pera, who keep my eyes on the road; Mike Thomas in Chicago, for his crack organizational skills and great cheer; Genelle Izumi-Uyekawa, who transcribed the words; David Rensin, for taking it on the chin; and especially the wonderful people and teachers of Andover, Massachusetts, who provided the bedrock for my life and, therefore, for this book.